Making the
Grass Greener
on Your Side

Making the Grass Greener on Your Side

A CEO's Journey to Leading By Serving

KEN MELROSE

Foreword by **Stephen R. Covey**

Berrett-Koehler Publishers
San Francisco

Berrett-Koehler Publishers, Inc.
155 Montgomery St.
San Francisco, CA 94104-4109
Tel: (415) 288-0260   Fax: (415) 362-2512

Ordering Information

Individual sales. Berrett-Koehler publications are available through most bookstores. They can also be ordered direct from Berrett-Koehler at the address above.

Quantity sales. Special discounts are available on quantity purchases by corporations, associations, and others. For details, contact the "Special Sales Department" at the Berrett-Koehler address above.

Orders for college textbook/course adoption use. Please contact Berrett-Koehler Publishers at the address above.

Orders by U.S. trade bookstores and wholesalers. Please contact Publishers Group West, 4065 Hollis Street, Box 8843, Emeryville, CA 94662. Tel: (510) 658-3453; 1-800-788-3123; Fax: (510) 658-1834.

Printed in the United States of America

 Printed on acid-free and recycled paper that is composed of 50% recovered fiber, including 10% post consumer waste.

Library of Congress Cataloging-in-Publication Data

Melrose, Ken, 1940-
 Making the grass greener on your side : a CEO's journey to leading by serving / Ken Melrose : foreword by Stephen R. Covery. — 1st ed.
  p. cm.
 Included bibliographical references and index.
 ISBN 1-881052-21-4 (alk. paper)
 1. Chief executive officers. 2. Leadership. 3. Industrial management. I. Title.
 HD38.2.M46 1995
 658.4--dc20   95-34423
                CIP

First Edition
99   98   97   96   95   10   9   8   7   6   5   4   3   2   1

For
Arrey, Peanut, and Tootely

This book is dedicated to all the women and
men of The Toro Company, "the wind beneath my wings."

. . . we must cultivate our garden.

— VOLTAIRE, CANDIDE

Contents

Foreword

by Stephen R. Covey
author of *The Seven Habits of Highly Effective People*

ONLY AN EXCEPTIONAL chief executive would subject himself voluntarily to internal scrutiny and external accountability, involving all the stakeholders of the organization. Ken Melrose, CEO of The Toro Company, is one such courageous executive. He's even posted his personal goals outside his office for all to see, along with an accounting of his performance against those goals.

Both his office and his mind are open, and people at all levels of the company are invited to share their ideas. He freely shares information in good times and bad, thus creating a culture of trust. By inviting peoples' involvement in whatever problems arise, he gains influence and earns their commitment. He tries to empower others, even in situations when it would be easier to do the task himself.

Ken and I believe that the key to effective delegation is to establish a clear, up-front mutual understanding and commitment regarding expectations in five areas:

Results Specify the quantity and quality of desired results.

Guidelines Focus on principles, not on procedures, policies, or practices.

Resources Identify available human, financial, and physical resources.

Accountability Schedule progress reports and specify performance criteria.

Consequences State both positive and negative rewards that reflect the natural consequences of actions taken.

I often refer to this system of management as the "win-win performance agreement." Another term I use is "stewardship delegation," since in such agreements each person becomes a "steward" over certain resources and responsibilities.

While I talk stewardship, Ken Melrose and his team at Toro walk it daily. His servant-leadership style and his sense of stewardship, not ownership, of his resources make him a model of what *Fortune* magazine calls "the new post-heroic leadership."

Green and Growing

As you might expect, Ken Melrose knows how to grow things—people, ideas, organizations. He follows natural laws and principles to keep things "green and clean." For many years, I've told my own green-and-clean story based on my experience in training one of my sons to care for our yard. Many times during that experience, I had to reaffirm within myself that my primary purpose was his character development. I was raising children, not grass. The yard was only a means to that end. After many false starts, my son finally signed the stewardship agreement deep within himself. It became his yard. He asked for help only two or three more times that summer. He had entered into a trust, a stewardship.

The same principle, of course, applies to Toro's business and to Melrose's system of management. In his book, we read many stories of Toro employees and others who understand that everyone in this company and culture, including the CEO, is subject to the same set of operating principles and guidelines—that this is a "farm" where natural laws govern, not a "school" nor "shop" where social, academic, and political rules govern.

Even in times of economic recession and hostile market conditions, Melrose and his leadership team at Toro have not sold out on matters of principle. Nor have they blamed their people. Rather they have stuck to their slow-but-sure growth strategies—preparing soil, planting seed, managing the turf, and harvesting fruits. This is agriculture applied to corporate culture.

Recently, Melrose has positioned Toro as an environmental company—not as some slick public relations ploy, but simply as the most accurate description of the vision and mission of the organization. This book documents the fact that Toro people, like the irrigation systems and lawn mowers they make, help us to create and maintain an environment we can take pride in. "Pride In Excellence," the nomenclature for their corporate culture, creates pride of ownership.

Ken Melrose manages The Toro Company on the basis of trust, daily making meaningful deposits into the emotional bank accounts of all stakeholders. Such deposits add up to a considerable sum because once people gain a sense of stewardship in an area of responsibility, and trust in their associates, they will faithfully perform their jobs to the best of their abilities with little or no supervision. Now, that's a return on investment!

The "good news" message in this marvelous book is that you and I can realize our own goals and dreams—and see our own "green-and-clean" results—by applying the timeless principles of effective leadership.

Acknowledgments

WHEN I BEGAN WRITING *Making the Grass Greener on Your Side,* I had no idea how much help I'd need and how many people would be involved. It began simply enough with Stephen Covey and Ken Shelton, Stephen's long-term friend and editor of *Executive Excellence,* talking with me about putting principle-centered leadership into practice—in a real, live corporation. The idea of writing about my experience as a servant leader of The Toro Company seemed straightforward enough, and the ideas and stories poured forth. But organizing it—putting it into a sensible structure and presenting it in book form—was rather overwhelming. And so over the long journey from start to finish, I enlisted many friends who happily and freely came to my aid.

Certainly, I cannot thank Ken Shelton enough. He helped with every aspect of the book, labored long with me as my partner, conceptualizing, interpreting, writing, and editing the many manuscripts. Without Ken, this book would never have been ventured much less written. Enormous thanks go also to Don Stolz of the Old Log Theatre and Ronn Lehmann, both of Minneapolis, for their counsel and many edits.

Lynde Sorensen, Jim Secord, and David McNally were extremely helpful in advising me on structure, content, and positioning. They had many useful ideas. In addition, I am particularly grateful to Harvey Mackay, who gave me hours of his precious time for helpful advice. Special thanks must also go to the many Toro employees who so willingly shared their stories and experiences. Deciding which stories to use in this book was one of my biggest challenges. As I read each one of them I was inspired and constantly reminded of the rich rewards of leading by serving. I owe them a debt of gratitude for helping some of the concepts and principles of servant leadership come alive through their real life experiences at Toro.

I had a host of readers who joyfully read, read, read, and then read some more. My heartfelt thanks to this merry band—Penny George, Carol Keers, Janet Hagberg, and Rob Melrose.

Last, but certainly not least, was the team in the trenches, behind their PCs, word processing indefatigably. They endured the tedious process of typing and retyping at all hours of the day over the entire project. My special thanks to Sharon Richards, Mim Rischmiller, Mary Buckeridge, and Colleen Steinhaus.

As their servant leader, I can claim unabashedly that these many friends exemplified a real, empowered team!

Introduction

The journey is better than the end.
— CERVANTES

To travel hopefully is a better thing than to arrive.
— ROBERT LOUIS STEVENSON

I'VE LEARNED IN LIFE that the journey is often as important as the destination. I've learned also that leadership continuously shapes and fashions an environment, and that environment can foster the growth of both the individual and the enterprise—or their demise. This book is about a journey, my own journey of self-analysis and personal discovery. This is not a journey for everyone, however, and probably is not even a journey for every leader. To successfully navigate down his or her own path, a leader must have a special mix of ingredients.

This work illustrates how one real-world corporation, The Toro Company, was jerked out of its business-as-usual routines and dropped on the road to bigger and better things. My intention is not to detail a personal history, nor Toro's history. The weave and color of the Toro tapestry will be revealed, however, because they create the framework within which some leadership lessons may be learned. I present a story about how I learned to practice leadership based on principles and on serving the organization, as that organization experienced prosperity and expansion as well as hardship and contraction. And I present a story about how a culture evolved to help create a stronger, more viable company.

Servant Leaders

The phrase that best describes the leadership style that I continue to strive for is *servant leadership,* as described by Robert Greenleaf in his book *Servant Leadership.* I say "continue to strive for" because the journey of leadership is about becoming, not attaining some final destination, and I still have a distance to go.

When I first read *Servant Leadership,* I didn't see how a business leader could "serve" all the stakeholders of the organization. But through the example of my brother, my parents, and others whom I admired, I began to see how true leaders served others and thus multiplied their skills and transferred their vision and values to others.

During the seventies, particularly when I was president of Game Time, a playground equipment manufacturer that was then a subsidiary of Toro, I came to realize that everyone in an organization has real value. Servant leaders don't just serve the competent, privileged, and advantaged people; they serve everyone because everyone has value and can make a meaningful contribution.

Later, in the eighties, when I mixed my belief in servant leadership with the principles of compassion, confidence, and courage, I set the foundation for a new style of "deep-rooted" leadership, the first rule being, "Do it because it's the right thing to do." I believe that an effective, deep-rooted leader is passionate about principles. The servant leader constantly draws on this passion to enrich lives, build better human beings, and encourage people to become more than they ever believed they could. More than a job or career, deep-rooted leadership is about having a mission.

When leaders model service, it becomes a master principle that flows throughout a corporate culture. The servant-leadership style promotes a more open, involved, trusting, spontaneous, and cooperative working environment. It permits—and requires—every team member to grow and develop, both personally and professionally. And better than other leadership models, it promotes opportunities for corporate success because people work and live best in a community where they genuinely serve each other's needs.

Service begets service; a positive cycle is created that gives an organization a long-term, sustainable, competitive edge. This competitive edge is a by-product of servant leadership, but it is not an end in itself. Servant leaders serve out of compassion and concern for people, and out of a desire to promote and celebrate every individual within their circle of influence.

Perhaps not surprisingly, the personality traits and character principles that I identify with servant leadership were developed in my early childhood from the ideals, standards, and beliefs I grew up with at home. My parents raised my brother and me according to their own principles, and those became our roots. As I grew up, though, I was only vaguely aware of the attitudes and ideals I admired in my parents. Unconsciously, I developed similar attitudes and ideals, and these ultimately created the style of leadership I would employ as president of The Toro Company many years later. However, as I passed through some of Toro's most difficult times, my commitment to servant leadership would be severely tested.

New Models of Leadership

Today's business literature mandates new models and styles of leadership and documents how these have evolved out of the changing roles and expectations of the American worker and customer. Social and economic changes over the last twenty years have wreaked havoc on the American corporate scene, causing massive restructuring, reengineering, consolidating, down sizing, right sizing, and all the rest.

Much of the response of American leaders to these upheavals has been tardy and reactive—perhaps because of difficulty in identifying and accepting the new realities created by the global marketplace. We all tend to hang on to the comfortable "old reality" that seems both more certain and more secure. We all prefer the familiar reality to one that arrives unannounced on the doorstep, full of rude surprises. Small wonder, then, that in spite of exhortations by such futurists as Alvin Toffler and John Naisbitt, America's business leaders have resisted emerging realities. Michael Crichton's story, *Jurassic Park,* which became a popular movie in 1993, is a dramatic case in point. The protagonist, John Hammond, tries unsuccessfully to merge the past with the present. The result is a new reality he could never have anticipated. Hammond creates dinosaurs from DNA extracted from ancient mosquito blood, and builds a self-contained (or so he thinks) park as a natural habitat for his creatures. When he experiences the calamitous results of mixing old and new forces, he learns that recreating the past is no way to succeed in today's world.

I was no more clairvoyant when we initiated a new company culture at Toro back in 1983. For me, it was a way to begin moving the company into alignment with the attitudes and practices that were rooted in my principles and leadership ideals. These were obviously much more clear to me, as was my vision for the company, and in hindsight, I grossly underestimated the amount of faith and courage others needed to draw on to follow my lead. I give a great deal of credit to the employees and the other Toro stakeholders who rode out those rough years with me. Crisis is often a thinly veiled mandate for change, and it certainly was the natural impetus for many of our decisions, and for many of the turns we took in our journey together.

The decision to embark down the path of servant leadership at Toro was made as we were coming out of our most traumatic period. The crisis—with its broad, deep, and expansive problems—forced us into a great deal of corporate self-analysis. As one member of the board of directors put it, "The patient was in the operating room, hemorrhaging profusely, and dying."

Just two years before, at the end of our fiscal year 1979, we had reached a pinnacle of unparalleled expansion and development. Sales had doubled and net earnings had more than tripled during that time. We had built or bought additional plants, hired new people, and added new departments as we continued to increase production and expand distribution. Our principal product lines were lawn mowers and snow throwers. Winters of blizzards and summer seasons of warm rainfalls had created a seemingly insatiable demand for Toro products.

Then, not "just one thing went wrong" at Toro—as theater marquees billed the movie *Jurassic Park*—but *everything* seemed to go wrong. There was virtually no snowfall in any of the world's snowbelts. A worldwide recession surfaced, fueled by rampant U.S. interest rates, which shot up to an unprecedented 20 percent. Despite this, the delusion of old realities and our momentum (which we erroneously believed we had single-handedly created) held us fast to our disastrous course. After a second winter of low snowfall, with the economy beginning to worsen, we found ourselves in dire straits. "Fiscal 1981" might better have been termed "Fiasco 1981." We lost over $13 million that year—our first loss since 1945.

Because we were teetering on a financial precipice, three of our largest banks canceled our lines of credit. Our public accounting firm debated long over giving us a qualified opinion. Many dealers were disgruntled and hurt financially by Toro's eroding product quality, our lack of focus and discipline, and our preoccupation with selling to the mass merchandisers. As a result, they shifted their selling emphasis to competing brands. Our sales fell precipitously: 50 percent over a two-year period. We were top-heavy with corporate managers, superfluous departments, and excessive staffs; this became glaringly evident when we compared our corporate overhead rates with those of our competitors.

The result was make-work, confusion, and low productivity. Morale hit an all-time low. The chairman and CEO terminated the president and COO, and then resigned two weeks later, seeking greener pastures. By the end of 1981, the only question became whether or not Toro could survive. The board of directors did not seek a "quick fix," but appointed a new and rather "green" management team to find a sound survival course that could also help Toro regain long-term market leader position.

Our dire circumstances forced us into a corporate self-examination. We came to realize that the only strategy able to satisfy our short-run requirements and provide future opportunities was a return to our fundamental strengths at the same time as seeding new growth using the greatest asset any company has: its people. We deliberately chose this more difficult "seed not sod" course, and ultimately, it was our salvation. It was not an easy ride, but as one who had been taught to resist the easy way out, I was grateful for the board's direction. It's course was to plant seeds, let them germinate, and grow solutions.

As we seeded our new culture, we struggled with many of the new realities of business: ever-increasing customer expectations, the emerging "horizontal" corporate structure, and the volatile world economy. We learned all the buzz phrases such as world-class manufacturing, total quality management, quality circles, paradigm shifting, cellular teams, and job ownership. More importantly, we learned about empowerment, trust, teamwork, recognition, shared rewards, open communications, celebrations, honesty, and synergy.

As a leader, I've learned that it isn't enough to read the right books and attend the latest seminars. We need to be honest and humane—to "walk the talk" day after day. We need to create an environment for personal and corporate success that allows for a natural growth process. We need to make the goals of management and employees refreshingly compatible and mutually attainable. Unless our goals are met together, they likely won't be met at all.

Those who embark on this quest for deep-rooted servant leadership will need special characteristics not found in all leaders, even "successful and proven" leaders. But to those who follow natural growth processes, a rich harvest awaits—not only at the journey's end, but also along the way.

Four Stages of Growth

I have divided this book into four parts—a section for each stage of the growth process. The section titles serve as an extended metaphor.

Section I: Preparing the Soil. This section refers to values and principles that we develop early in life or that we recognize and adopt through life experience. These principles keep us true to our course, even in times of dire need. They enable us to weather the storm; they keep us "clean and green," even when we are tempted to relax or opt for a more expedient, opportunistic quick fix.

Section II: Seed Not Sod. This section embodies the creation of a vision that moves across boundaries and pushes us toward new paradigms. In creating a vision of what might be, we do not accept things as they are but persevere through continuous improvement, knowing that we (and our companies) can always be better than the current reality would have us believe. Our vision sets the direction the journey will take for the individual, team, and organization.

Section III: Managing and Maintaining the Turf. This section recognizes the cycles, processes, standards, and systems involved in managing a business. In managing our turf, we believe in being tenacious and accountable for results. We don't give up but rather get up each day and say, "I'm a little closer to that goal, but need to pull myself and the organization up by the bootstraps. I can't let that goal out of my sights."

Section IV: The Harvest. This final section explores the rich fruits of the harvest. Preparing the soil, seeding instead of sodding, and wisely managing turf yields an abundant harvest. If you have built a competitive team—one that leverages results, sustains growth, continually improves its health, reaches for its potential, and is flexible, adaptive, always learning—you will find that what you at first struggled to accomplish now occurs spontaneously during your never-ending journey.

You will also find that the fruits of the harvest transcend the good of the company because you yourself have become a better person. You will have confirmed that leadership has the privilege and the responsibility to bring full dimension to people's lives. Together you and your employees will have made your company a community—a family—that nurtures and fosters each other to a greater degree of wholeness in a worthy endeavor. Together you will have fulfilled a meaningful purpose.

These environmental metaphors come directly from the fabric of Toro. The outdoor environment is our domain. We plant, irrigate, fertilize, mow, recycle, compost, aerate, cut, edge, trim, and vacuum all lawns, big and small. To have a healthy lawn, you must do all of this, as well as hope for warm seasons with sunshine and rainfall. You grow a healthy organization the same way. That's why growing grass is a fitting metaphor for growing an organization. This environmental metaphor suggests:

SOIL PREPARATION + SEEDING + SOUND TURF MANAGEMENT = HARVEST

These are the building blocks that lead to the desired results. Leadership is the instrument that makes it happen.

The conclusions and reflection in this book are mine, formed from my own impressions and sensitivities and out of my own experiences. Some Toro employees who read this book may think I've taken liberties, or my recollection of things has faded. But I don't expect my impressions to be the same as those of others who watched or experienced the same events from a different position. We are all unique human beings, fashioned out of different fabrics with different backgrounds. Our unique sensibilities, attitudes, and values create a variety of conclusions and interpretations. I can only warrant that my report of what happened to me and to the corporation is as I saw it and felt it. These chapters reflect my experiences at Toro as best I can recall them. Many Toro employees volunteered to share stories of their own; unfortunately, I could not include them all. But I believe those you will read in the pages that follow provide a good representation of the spirit of our organization and culture. In matters of the heart, however, there's always room for subjectivity and different perceptions.

My hope is that everyone who reads this book will have a better understanding and a stronger dedication to creating environments for personal and business success, and to promoting the growth of the individual within that environment for the benefit of all. I challenge you, the reader, to find the courage within yourself to pursue and reach the future you desire for yourself and your organization. Only by reaching down within yourself to find those deep-rooted principles and ideals will you find the stamina and fortitude to weather the storms you will certainly encounter along your way.

As I struggle with inevitable change, countervailing forces, and the ever-changing realities of business, the image of the British Olympic gold-medal runner, Eric Liddell, comes to mind. Liddell's extraordinary dedication to his goals, his personal motivation, and the source of this strength were vividly portrayed in the film *Chariots of Fire.*

In his race for the gold medal in the 400-meter dash, he tired at the three-quarter point only to find a new strength that gave him the burst of speed he needed to win. The film won the Oscar for best picture of the year. The Academy could have awarded it for that one scene alone.

Like all champions, Liddell was asked by others, "Where did you find the power?" His reply was both simple and profound: "From within." And that must be our answer, too.

Preparing the Soil

LEELAND ALBERT DURR stood atop the hillock overlooking the farm that had just become his. Along with the farm came the responsibility to cultivate, to plant, and to nurture the land in a way that would bring the joy of the harvest to him and his family. He had looked forward to this moment of challenge for a long time. Directly before him was the field, now *his* field. It was the area he had determined would best suit the crop he would plant and be most likely to produce a fulsome harvest.

Lee had given years in preparation for this point in time—boyhood years working the family farm, studying agriculture and agronomy at school, and finally carefully studying the soil on this particular farm. He had evaluated the soil, received professional opinions from university experts, assessed its potential, and come to know its promise.

As he stood there, Lee reminded himself how fortunate for him that it was the fall of the year. Had it been spring, he might have rushed into planting without properly preparing the soil. Since it was autumn, he would not even be tempted to shortcut what he knew to be the proper process.

The experts had recommended a light application of lime in early fall. He would follow this with a broadcast fertilizer using a mixture that emphasized nitrogen combined with some phosphorous and potash. Knowing the light texture of the soil, Lee knew that the fertilized area would need to be tilled. In late winter, as the snow melted and its resultant moisture drained, he would grade the area. When early spring arrived, he would only need to apply a starter nutrient and regrade the areas that may have settled. He would then be ready to plant.

All of his experiences, his learning, and his insights from others had brought him to and prepared him for this specific moment. Now it was his responsibility to take his knowledge and apply it. Now it was his opportunity to experience his dream, to begin his journey, the journey leading to the harvest.

Successful leaders of the nineties and beyond are more and more frequently leading from a set of principles. They are finding that being principle centered stands the test of time and best weathers the storms of the economy and the marketplace, as well as the rapid changes, the complexities, and the chaos in today's enterprise. Building your leadership model on a solid foundation of principles is essential for long-term growth.

The process of building such a foundation begins by taking stock of where you are, by assessing your vision and values, and by grounding yourself in your principles. The next step is to become a self-starter, a principle-centered leader on your turf. The final step in building a solid foundation is to translate your principles to the rest of your management team, creating an organizational culture that reflects these principles and fosters deep-rooted growth.

CHAPTER ONE

Groundwork
for Growth

The greatest discovery of our generation is that human beings, by changing the inner attitudes of their minds, can change the outer aspects of their lives.
— ANONYMOUS

Expedients are for the hour; principles for the ages.
— H. W. BEECHER

LEADERSHIP IS NOT ABOUT *being*. Leadership is about *becoming*. Leadership is dynamic and active, always changing, always growing. In describing spiritual growth, St. Francis of Assisi wrote: "There is always more growing yet to come, and more light yet to shine." So too with leaders—there is always more growth and more light yet to come. But the journey must begin somewhere. It can begin by taking stock of where you are: your skills, your talents, and most importantly, your beliefs about leadership. Understanding yourself is the first step in deciding what kind of leader you want to become.

An important experience in shaping what kind of leader I wanted to be occurred in 1973. I was thirty-two at the time and found myself in Michigan, the newly appointed president of Game Time, Inc., a recent acquisition by The Toro Company. Game Time manufactured and marketed playground equipment for the commercial and institutional market. The company had revenues of less than $10 million and about two hundred employees, many of whom lived (and worked) on nearby farms. I was coming from a role in marketing lawn mowers and knew little or nothing about the business of playground equipment.

Different people had "helped" me build preconceptions about the Game Time company, its plant, and the small rural town in which it was located. I presumed that the environment was not very sophisticated and that the company's culture and management practices were much simpler than those at Toro. The Game Time employees had their preconceptions about me, too. The head office at Toro had told them to expect a Princeton graduate with advanced degrees from MIT and the University of Chicago. I don't know who was more uncomfortable that first day—they or I.

Before I arrived, Game Time had been run by its founder, a man I would describe as a benevolent dictator. We'll call him Bill. I didn't know what my leadership style was or exactly what it would be a week after I arrived, but I knew one thing: Bill's leadership style and mine were worlds apart.

During Bill's tenure, or more appropriately, Bill's *reign,* the people at Game Time had learned that Bill made the decisions—*all* the decisions. He liked to be involved in every aspect of the business. There were reasons for this, of course. Game Time had been Bill's company. He started it and he knew everything there was to know about building playground equipment. Regardless of the question, Bill always had an answer. There was no doubt about it; Bill was the boss.

The problem was that Bill's management style had taught his people to wait for him to tell them what to do. As a result, they did not exhibit much initiative in their jobs. During my first few weeks with the company, employees would walk into my office and ask for advice. For example, I might have been asked, "How much steel should we purchase?" "Should I ship this order or that order first?" "In what magazines should we advertise?" I didn't know the answers to those questions, but I knew how to find them.

"How much steel should we purchase?" the purchasing manager would ask.

"I don't know," I'd say. "How much steel did you buy in the last period?"

"Oh, thirty tons."

"Why did you buy that quantity?"

"Well," he'd say, "that's how much we needed to build one hundred merry-go-rounds."

"Okay. How many merry-go-rounds do we need to build this next period?"

After checking with the sales manager, he'd come back and tell me, "We've sold eighty. We'd better buy enough to build eighty merry-go-rounds."

"What about any extra orders that we may get?"

"Oh, right. Maybe we'd better have some in reserve."

"Is ten enough to have in reserve?" I'd ask.

"Yeah, that should be enough. We need enough steel to build ninety."

Then I'd say, "Well, maybe you should buy nine-tenths of the steel you bought when you were going to build one hundred."

"Oh, I see how you got that," he'd say. "Yeah, nine-tenths of our last order is enough to build ninety this period. That makes sense."

"But you'd better check with the plant manager to see what we have in stock, and back that out of the number. So next period, you'll know how to figure out how much steel we need."

"Sure, I can do that."

Over the three years I worked at Game Time, much of my effort was spent helping people learn processes for problem solving and decision making related to their jobs. What happened was quite revealing. As the people who had the knowledge, experience, and information began to solve problems and make their own decisions, they began to enjoy their work more. We made mistakes at first, but we learned together. People didn't get fired or chewed out; rather, they simply used the mistakes to learn and to get better. My fledgling leadership role created a learning environment. Together, we became more confident in our jobs and we developed more trust in each other. The bonds that formed allowed us to work as a team. We learned to accept and rely on our interdependence. We all grew in self-esteem and self-actualization, and in teaching others, I was the one who learned the most.

Soon after my Game Time experience, I read *Servant Leadership* by Robert Greenleaf. As the title suggests, the book is about leading an organization by serving it, not by directing or controlling it. Greenleaf's leadership model resonated with me as I reflected on my experience at Game Time. In my own crude way, I had tried to serve the people at Game Time in a way that made them better. For me, the Game Time environment was a servant-leadership prototype. It was an experiment in empowerment that gave me an actual experience of "leader as servant." Bit by bit, I came to understand that you lead best by serving the needs of your people. You don't do their jobs for them; you enable them to learn and progress on the job. You multiply strengths as you empower and trust. When you do, you invariably find that what limits the contribution of people is more their work culture and norms than their abilities. Create an environment for personal growth, and people rise to their potential.

It was gratifying to see that principles such as loyalty, service, interdependence, and empowerment—principles I'd been brought up with and had come to value personally—actually worked. I agree with the old proverb: "Give a man a fish, and you feed him for a day. Teach him to fish, and you feed him for a lifetime." I learned at Game Time that teaching people how to fish is wise—it benefits not only the employees but also the corporation. By the time we sold the company three years later, Game Time's sales had increased 50 percent, profits had more than doubled, and the company was yielding the best return on investment of all Toro's divisions.

The Upward Climb

My experiences at Game Time also taught me how important it is to step back every now and then to look at what you're doing with your life. I came to understand that my core beliefs, principles, and values are at the heart of what I do and why I do it. If we are to become wise stewards of our company's future, we must begin by carefully assessing our core beliefs, principles, and values. This is not a one-time assignment. Periodic self-assessment helps us understand where we are, where we're going, and why. It also helps us understand the impact of our beliefs and behaviors on others. And it's the best way to grow as a person.

Progress from one growth level to the next requires you to continually reach down within yourself to find and unleash new power and to open new perspectives, with commitment and passion. Progress means tapping your inner strengths and sharing with others the power and spirit you discover. Each day I try to take on the challenge of making at least one thing better. It may be dealing with the person who irritated me the day before, attempting to solve a nagging problem at the office, or a personal issue that I've been avoiding.

When you set out to accomplish things, you discover there are no easy resolutions to the challenges of life and leadership, especially when the process depends on self-discovery. I do think, though, that this is an important starting point. If you take time to consciously consider your own life experience, to think about your values and how those values influence your daily activities and relate to your work, you'll be engaging in what Toro's Irrigation Division describes as deep watering.

For me, this self-renewal includes running every day, which combines strenuous physical exertion with quiet reflection on absorbing issues. Usually, I return physically exhausted but mentally recharged, filled with new ideas. Often, I focus on those things that will move the organization to new heights and me closer to my leadership purpose. In addition, this personal time gives me a sense of self-maintenance. I'm taking care of myself. The opportunity for introspection, combined with the discipline of running, gives me the conviction that I can generate the necessary energy to make some progress in my life.

I wonder how many of us can articulate our beliefs and values. How many could sit down with another person and explain honestly and clearly what our standards and values are, without hesitation, apology, or discomfort? This is difficult enough in our private lives, and I think it's even more difficult in business—a point supported by the organizational behavioralists. As a matter of fact, some experts in the field believe that most people don't act according to their espoused principles. How much more difficult it must be for the person who has never given conscious, quality effort to defining what those principles are!

I challenge you to make time in your day to pause and identify the guiding principles of your life. Hopefully, defining your values and principles concretely will enable you to take more overt ownership and integrate them into your daily life. You'll have a rare chance to honestly examine your values, principles, and beliefs, to hold them up against your personal models, and to determine their worth and suitability in what you do.

Self-assessment and personal development aren't easy. I like to think about this process in terms of rock climbing. Picture yourself with both feet firmly planted on the ground, looking up the vertical face of a mountain. Your goal is somewhere over your head, possibly even out of your view, but you know what it is. Because the ascent is perpendicular and there are few outcroppings to support you, you know the climb will be difficult. But with the right equipment, with skill, and with determination, you can make it. If you're lucky, others will have gone before you and left pitons in place—stanchions that, with your ropes, will support you if you slide or fall backward in your upward climb. Every climb begins with a reach and step toward your goal; if you don't understand where you're starting from, you can never be sure of your progress.

The next step in rock climbing is to know where you want to go. In leadership, this means setting goals—knowing what you want to become and why. Goal-setting is more than a "mental exercise"; it requires confidence and commitment. Maxwell Maltz, author of *Psycho-cybernetics,* found that people could dramatically change the outer aspects of their lives by changing their mental attitudes. In effect, our thoughts can shape our lives. Our inner lives, or our thoughts and predispositions, determine the behaviors and habits that characterize our outer lives. In fact, the external is a mirror reflection of the internal. In other words, we become what we choose. Thus, when we commit to a goal with the belief that we can achieve it, we improve our chances immeasurably.

As a leader, your job is to provide direction and bring about positive change. Until you know where you are and where you want to go, you can't do your job. As the saying goes, "If you don't know where you're going, any road will get you there." Self-assessment eliminates needless drift by providing a picture of where you are and where you want to be. You can then set your goals and keep on target.

Self-analysis requires you to proactively seek feedback. Seeking and accepting feedback require courage. You must take a hard look at your beliefs about people, define yourself in terms of your principles, measure your behavior against those principles, and recognize when you come up short.

The leader's role is then to carry such analysis a step further: from *what is* to *what can be.* I believe human beings have a great capacity for growth. Without faith and vision, however, growth isn't possible. Faith and vision, two key elements of leadership, build the belief that we can improve, and they sustain our efforts to improve. The desire to change can be transient or long lasting. What makes the difference between a New Year's resolution that fades over the following weeks and a renewal of spirit and soul that changes our lives forever? Vision, faith, purpose, dedication, and courage. Each is a step upward, toward the goal that is perhaps out of sight but still attainable.

A Personal Equation for Success

When I was a child, my mother drilled into me the attitude, "Never give up; try again." I'm sure that attitude has contributed to my perseverance. Countless times, my mother read me the children's story *The Little Engine That Could.* Her voice repeating "I think I can, I think I can" will live with me always—a constant reminder of a simple formula: a positive attitude plus a clear goal equals an increased probability of success. Creating that attitude within your organization will improve your chances of reaching your goal.

For most of us our parents are our first heroes, our first and most powerful role models. Children identify with their family groups and learn behavior from them. Church, school, and television may also be powerful influences, but the family core comes first. Despite the sad and sobering picture Bill Bennett, former U.S. Secretary of Education, portrays of the weakening fabric of our society in *The Index of Leading Cultural Indicators,* the family is still the primary source of values—good and bad—that influence us throughout our lives, whatever else we learn on our journey.

You've seen children at play. They pretend to be cowboys, or doctors, or astronauts. They imagine themselves in different roles, just as we did when we were children. In psychology, this is called "modeling," and while we normally associate it with children, we in fact do it all our lives. As adults we practice the behaviors we think are appropriate for the roles we desire; we observe the behaviors of people we admire, and oftentimes their behaviors become our behaviors. That's how junior managers become senior managers, and how would-be-CEOs eventually move into the real role. The leader influences this process by enabling others to visualize what they want to become and by convincing them that they are on their way.

After considerable reflection, I came to believe that the values and beliefs I had been brought up with as a child—values such as perseverance, loyalty, excellence, and service to others—were valid not only in my personal life but also in the workplace. They are the foundation of such leadership attributes as trust, empowerment, and commitment. At Game Time, I learned that I could base my leadership style on these values and enable people to grow and make greater contributions. People who are empowered to do what is right, I discovered, make better business decisions and contribute to one another's growth and development. The by-product is a productive, confident workforce.

The following story is one of many told in this book by people who have worked with me. I have included these stories for two reasons: first, they help document the changes and events at Toro; and second, they tell the story best. This account by Anne Waldherr is an example of what can happen when people are given the opportunity, in the right environment, to thrive and grow both personally and professionally.

I STARTED AT TORO in February of 1991 as an administrative assistant. Although I enjoyed secretarial work, I knew I had more to offer this company in another capacity. The policy of Toro to post job openings internally is the reason I am where I am today.

I went after a job titled associate merchandising representative, and due to Mr. Scott Barlass, director of Consumer Marketing, I was promoted to the Marketing Department in January of 1993. Scott told me later that he saw something in me and my abilities that he felt would make a contribution to his team. Because I was allowed to bloom and grow, I feel my contributions to Toro will grow as well. When I was given the job in marketing, I was encouraged to pursue the college degree that I left unfinished in 1980. I plan to graduate in the spring of 1996.

If more companies encouraged their employees to strive for excellence and achieve their highest potential, they'd be much more successful.

—Anne Waldherr

See what I mean by confident? When people are empowered, they exude confidence. They know where they are and where they're going, so they don't worry about knowing exactly how to get there. But in order to reach their goals and to achieve excellence, they must have standards. Enhancing the performance capability of people like Anne Waldherr is one of the best investments a company can make.

Standards of Excellence

Here's a story of my own that illustrates the importance of standards:

A TWELVE-YEAR-OLD BOY banged the side door shut as he came home from school on a day that beckoned winter. It was the end of his first school term, and among his books was his report card.

Later that evening, he sat quietly in the living room, watching as his father studied the grades with a grimace and a furrowed brow. Before his father could say anything, the boy nervously blurted out, "The teacher said I did okay."

The father handed the card to the mother, and before she too could show her disappointment, the boy added, half optimistically this time, "The teacher said I was in the top half of my class."

After a lengthy pause, his father began to speak. "Son," he said gently, but sternly, "you shouldn't be so concerned with how well you did compared to the other students, or even how your teacher felt about your marks. What's important—far more important—is that you set a standard of excellence for yourself. That standard will become the measure that tells you if you did your very best, and will enable you to look back at all you do without regret. It's a standard that will challenge the very best in you. And always remember, it can't be the teacher's standard nor anyone else's. It must be yours, and yours alone. You have to own it."

I first heard this story when I was fourteen years old. My family was gathered at Princeton University to celebrate the graduation of my older brother, Bob. I was so proud that Bob was one of those receiving the high honors conferred that day. I remember looking at my parents and being surprised at the tears streaming down their faces. I didn't know until later that Bob had been the boy in this story.

We were there on that bright June day partly because of the lesson our parents had given to Bob years ago, and partly because, from our parent's example, Bob had set himself a standard of excellence. Our parents planted in Bob and in me the seeds of a model of excellence—one based on a set of principles. They believed in our infinite capacity for self-improvement, and eventually we believed in it too. Still, we, by our own actions, had to make the standard of excellence part of the fabric of our lives.

Each of us has that capacity for self-improvement. As leaders, we have the responsibility to inspire and guide others to live up to their potential. To do that, we have to model the character and behavior we hope to see in others. Leadership is an inside-out thing—what we have internalized, we reflect outwardly in what we do. Lip service accomplishes nothing. No matter what our talk may be, it is our walk, our behavior, that reveals our true beliefs.

When we honestly walk our talk, we link our beliefs and our behaviors. There's congruence between the two because why we do something is as important as what we do. Both beliefs and behaviors are integral parts of our character. Those people who say one thing and do another have failed to achieve this integrity. Regardless of what they say, their behavior will betray them because the behavior is ultimately the product of their beliefs.

Sometimes leaders don't recognize the incongruence between their words and actions. Open and honest self-assessment, conducted regularly and realistically, can help us find incongruencies, see where we fall short of our goals, show us where we are, and point us in the direction we would like to go. When we recognize incongruence between our words and behaviors, we need to reconcile that incongruence before we can break ground for the new growth needed to reach the goals we've targeted. These goals are like mile-markers along the roads we choose to travel; they serve as checkpoints for our journey. Standards of excellence focus and channel our best efforts, and along the way we grow and become stronger.

Examining the Soil

Potential exists in everything, but potential is also a matter of perception and choice. A common red brick can be the cornerstone of a structure that will withstand the elements for decades, protecting generation after generation within its walls. The same red brick can be a weapon, a flying object of destruction and pain.

We, too, become what we choose to be. Potential is the distance between what we are today and what we can become. I've always been struck by the words of Ashley Montagu: "The deepest personal defeat suffered by human beings is constituted by the difference between what one was capable of becoming and what one has in fact become."

Since the leader's journey is one of both individual and corporate discovery, it must include an examination of soil and roots. I believe the images that preoccupy us—our beliefs, our values, our goals—reflect the soil in which the seeds of our future will be sown. Our visions are either positive or negative. The level of confidence we have in ourselves tells us what we can—or can't—achieve. The mind can be our best friend or our worst enemy. The choice is ours. Who we are and who we're capable of becoming are questions that we must answer within ourselves.

From the time I returned to Toro to run the Outdoor Power Equipment Division, after we sold Game Time in 1976, until I became Toro's president in 1981, I grappled with these questions of values and choices. It was a period of great financial success for the company, fueled in large part by an inflationary economy and agreeable weather patterns. It was also a period of floundering and frustration for me as I tried to replicate my experiences at Game Time in my new arena. My leadership principles and cultural values were not aligned with others in the Toro management ranks. Managing a division just down the hall from the corporate offices was difficult to do against a different philosophy about people, but I naively let my values lead my actions.

For example, I organized a small group of Toro managers and leaders to meet informally each Friday morning before the workday began. Our agenda was to exchange ideas on applying ethical business and employee relationship practices that encouraged managers to value people processes as well as end results. I don't believe I made much of a dent in the way Toro did things, but it taught me the power that the company head has in setting the operating tone and style of the organization.

Then, in the midst of the recession in 1981, as the company's earnings were sinking along with morale, I became president of The Toro Company. All at once, it was my job to address questions of who we were, where we were going, and what we could achieve. I was forced to examine the soil and to initiate some dramatic changes. In that first year, we cut almost half of our total office staff; and yet we still struggled to survive through the next year. The reductions reminded us that "downsizing" is a euphemism for eliminating people and jobs because we were not good stewards in the past. We could only hope to find a way to do it with compassion.

To get our financial structure in line with the new realities of our business prospects and to satisfy the expectations of banks and shareholders, we needed a comprehensive overhaul of our entire organization and mind-set. Prior to making any eliminations, we formed two independent employee teams and assigned each of them the task of developing a new organization with a targeted number of employees filling only essential job positions. The two teams and I then worked together to determine the positions that would support the business we anticipated through our recovery. Where the two teams agreed, I supported their recommendations; where they differed, we worked together to find consensus.

We then reviewed the potential contribution of every employee with regard to seniority, creativity, ability, past performance, and compatibility with the emerging culture and vision. We offered outplacement services for those people we let go, providing them with a phone contact office, assistance from an administrative staff, counseling, aptitude testing, a retraining facility, and fair severance packages. We did what we did because if we wanted to survive, we had no choice. And we did it the way we did it because any other way would have been contrary to our principles.

For the next six months, our management team discussed what kind of company we wanted to be as well as what kind of company we did not want to be, and how we were going to get there. This corporate self-analysis led to a deep restructuring of roles, responsibilities, and relationships with one another, with our jobs, and with our company. Our concentrated effort forged a new belief system referred to as the "four core values," which formed the base of our emerging culture, which we named Pride In Excellence.

We were fortunate. *I* was fortunate. Although the road that led to our recovery, to financial health, and to a new corporate culture was paved in an environment of crisis and desperation, that road led to opportunity for future growth. Obviously, we had to make hard choices and major changes, but we tried to be faithful to the value system we wanted to live by. Our intent was to use our "red bricks" to lay a new foundation, not to hurt our displaced people. Examining the soil thus set the stage for our future growth.

Groundbreaking and Soil Preparation

One of the keys to Toro's survival in the eighties was having the courage to redefine who and what we were. Redefinition allowed us to choose what we would become. Previously, we had defined ourselves as a company that made and sold lawn mowers and snow throwers. As we moved toward the nineties, we began to reposition Toro as an environmental company. We were prepared to do a great deal of groundbreaking and soil preparation. We knew it might be as many as twenty years or more before we succeeded in our long-term goal of educating others to see us as more than merely "the lawn mower company." This gave us a new context for viewing our core beliefs, principles, and values. It also gave us new insights on how to redefine our corporate culture. Because we chose to redefine why and how we would act, we empowered ourselves to build our new culture.

Still, it wasn't easy. The new climate we envisioned did not progress as fast as we had hoped. In fact, after a decade, we still had a long way to go. Even today, we are still in the process of becoming. When we defined ourselves as an outdoor environment-focused company, we had to take a longer view of things. We had to transform the company at a human level. Gardeners and farmers understand that there is a natural, self-paced process to most things. They realize that this process can't be denied. We eventually came to understand that there is a basic truth in the equation:

SOIL PREPARATION + SEEDING + SOUND TURF MANAGEMENT = HARVEST

This equation has paid off for us as well as for our customers. You don't get the fruits without good roots, as the following account illustrates.

DON CLEMENS was hired as the superintendent at Blackwolf Run Golf Course, a Pete Dye-designed course in Kohler, Wisconsin, in 1987. Don was hired after the irrigation equipment was purchased and delivered, but before it was installed. The decision had been made to purchase equipment manufactured by Rainbird. Because of Don's experience with Toro at two previous golf courses, he asked the owners to return their new system and buy Toro irrigation equipment, which they did. The course opened for play in 1989, and in its first year of eligibility was ranked number thirty-one on *Golf Digest's* list of America's one hundred greatest golf courses.

In the summer of 1989, Don was a speaker at a Wisconsin superintendent's meeting. In his presentation to eighty superintendents, he said, "I hope that when making buying decisions, you all understand the importance of supporting the Toros of the world—the companies that spend money on research and development—and not the 'me-toos' or 'will-fitters' who only copy other companies. If you don't support the Toros of the world, they won't have the money, or they won't be here to spend the money, for research and development to further improve equipment to allow us to maintain our golf courses."

When I hear that from a customer, I know our formula is right—not just because it works for us but because it follows the natural laws.

Natural Laws

Most of us know what it's like to put off doing work until the last minute. Do you remember when you "pulled an all-nighter" that somehow got you through a final exam in school? Or waited until the weekend to prepare a Monday morning presentation from scratch? Can you imagine a farmer doing the same thing? Of course not! If the farmer skips a vital element in the equation, or compresses the process unnaturally, no amount of effort will make up for work neglected or short-circuited during the natural cycle of the planting and growing season. Natural laws are patterns of nature and life that have proven over time to be valid. They operate regardless of our understanding or our observance of them. Among these natural laws is the law of the harvest: We reap what we sow. Or we fail to reap what we have not sown well.

Part of our business at Toro is to build the equipment used to groom and maintain golf courses. I'm well aware that golf courses don't spring into being overnight. Rather, those carefully contoured fairways and greens and precisely cut grasses are the result of extraordinary and uncompromising preparation. Two or three years before the first golf club is swung, the course has to be designed and the soil readied. The shaping and sculpting of the land, the mounds, the swales, the traps—all require changing what was there into the architect's vision of what it might become. This isn't an easy task. It involves trucking in tons of dirt and sand, building lakes where none stood before, moving and adding trees, and using bulldozers and other heavy equipment to create hills, slopes, and mounds. And then, because the finished product must endure continuous and long-term wear, the grass has to be grown from seed.

Seeds scattered at random on unprepared ground rarely find the conditions they require to grow and develop. Preparedness (or groundbreaking) is both a time-honored principle and a necessity. Fresh ideas and concepts, like new seed, require newly tilled ground, fertilizer, water, sunshine, and careful cultivation, all in abundance. My job at Toro was to enlist the help and support of the management team to prepare the soil for the planting we wanted to do, and then to nurture the growth of buds and shoots that might otherwise be choked by weeds or die from lack of care.

More Soil Preparation

Breaking ground during a time of stress and recovery, in the aftermath of the early eighties, meant believing that we could create our own opportunities even against long odds. We had to recognize opportunities in the face of adversity. When we were faced with yet another layoff, we knew the only way to handle it was to keep a clear focus on the "end in sight," and move through the process as quickly as we could. It forced us to prioritize. We had to make decisions about what could and couldn't be done. We had to make tough choices, because we knew that we couldn't "do it all." We didn't have the luxury of time or extensive resources to insure survival.

Not everyone in our corporate offices agreed on what was essential. Everyone had his or her own perceptions of the problems and solutions, and yet we couldn't afford to get bogged down with accommodating everyone's wishes. That's why we have leaders: to make effective but expedient decisions and keep the enterprise on course. Our leadership decisions positioned Toro to take advantage of the opportunities within economic recovery.

We began to reposition Toro as an environmental company in the late eighties. Our mission: to become, by the year 1999, the pre-eminent marketer and worldwide provider of products, services, and systems for the preservation and enhancement of the outdoor environment. We were prepared to do a great deal of groundbreaking and soil preparation. We knew it might be years before we succeeded in our long-term goal of educating others to see us as more than merely "the lawn mower company."

Why, then, did we embark on selling ourselves as a company bent on improving the outdoor environment when we could hardly keep our heads above water? Because we were breaking ground and planting seeds for the future. We were committing ourselves to an organic viewpoint. We chose to promote a culture that demonstrates our commitment to our deepest values. We chose to focus on products that preserve or enhance the environment. We chose to be environmentally sound in what we do and create ways for our people to participate in the care of their own environments. We chose to break ground for new growth on both a personal and corporate level.

To accomplish our goals, we had to be smarter than the competition; we had to look at every challenge as an opportunity. Fresh ideas and new concepts were essential. We needed more than just positive thinking. We enabled people to see opportunities and to use initiative and innovation to take advantage of those opportunities. Newly tilled ground was required to give the seeds a chance to germinate and take root. We had toiled and cultivated the soil and selected the seed. Our growth was underway.

One year we introduced a new snow thrower that completely sold out its production in the first year. Another year we introduced a little hand-held lawn vacuum. In today's economy, many companies enjoy an increasingly larger contribution to their growth and success from new products. For example, half of Hewlett Packard's sales in recent years have been from products that were less than three years old. In our case, we target 30 percent of our revenues to come from products that have been introduced within the previous three years.

To introduce our hand-held vacuum blower, we used an advertisement that showed Toro taking on all the competition by joining two vacuums snout to snout and then starting them up. Every time, the Toro bag bellowed out with the air from the competitor's bag as it collapsed. We literally sucked the air right out of the competition. The right execution of the right ideas will do the same to the competition every time. In good times or bad, you can take the wind right out of their sails if you're committed to your goal and determined to see it through.

Preparation is essential, whether it means readying the ground for seed or determining developmental essentials for a new product. At Toro, our best new products are the ones for which we did our homework in the beginning. Prevention, maintenance, and some pioneering in R&D—also types of groundbreaking—don't often get the accolades they deserve, however, because their work isn't seen as spectacular.

We sometimes forget how important prevention and preparation are. They tend to get separated from the end success because there's a long road between the product development team that comes up with an innovation or a new product, and the sales success of a year or more later. At the time of the sales launch, the engineers who, two years earlier, worked on the innovative design, the structural analysis, the prototyping, the testing, and the debugging are now working on a new group of products. Be careful not to focus your attention and recognition on the sales department only, just because the new product is boosting sales by a handsome percent.

We need recognition systems that equally value the talents and contributions of all members of a team, whether in groundbreaking, weeding the rows, or harvesting the crop planted so long ago by other hands. This is critical for improving the effectiveness of the team. John Cowan writes in *Small Decencies:*

> WHEN OUR LIVES are lived in service to the organization, should not the organization provide for the solemn moments? My suggestion is a book of ceremonies, expressing the company feelings at times of passage. . . . Each ceremony would express the corporation's gratitude for the gift of time from a human life, the one thing that once given can never be taken back. . . . Our accomplishments are not too simple, mundane, and ordinary to merit a moment of glory. We deserve to have our fellow workers sing our song. We owe them a poem in their honor.

We owe the team a system that demonstrates by action and response that every individual's efforts are important components in the company's success.

I believe the company that accepts the responsibilities and executes the philosophy I have described here—genuinely and with excellence—will succeed eventually, if not immediately. When leaders examine where they are, where they wish to be, and commit to directing the company's growth, then they will achieve its goals. Faith, vision, and hard work result in the outcomes we desire. In the framework of servant leadership, it's a definitive equation that allows us to play out our core beliefs, principles, and values in what we do and why we do it.

CHAPTER TWO

Be a
Self-Starter

Guaranteed to start, or we'll fix it free!
— TORO MARKETING SLOGAN

THE ABILITY TO BE a "self-starter" has been recognized for years as an important leadership trait. And yet there are days when even strong leaders don't want to get out of bed. Here's an illustration of my point.

IT'S EARLY MORNING and Johnny is still in bed. His mother calls him from the base of the stairs, "Johnny, you've got to get up; it's time to go to school!" He yells back downstairs, "No, I want to stay in bed." "Johnny," she says, "you have to get up. You've got to go to school. You're going to be late."

Finally she comes upstairs, but he's fallen asleep again. She shakes him until he sits up. "Johnny," she says, "get out of bed." Johnny replies, "I don't want to go to school today." His mother asks, "Why not?" "The problems are too hard, people don't like my ideas, and it seems like I have to please everyone," he tells her.

"Johnny," says his mother, "You simply have to go to school today." "Why do I have to go to school today?" he asks. "Well, for one thing," she says, "you're forty-two years old, and for another, you're the principal."

I can relate to that. The beginning of the day is the hardest time for me. I'm a "night owl," and I don't bounce out of bed in the early morning with great exuberance. When the alarm wakes me up, I lie there collecting my thoughts and reviewing my plan of action for the day. However, I realize that nothing is going to happen until I get up. Once I get going, I begin to focus on the day's opportunities. Then I'm dressed, out of the house, and off to work; soon I'm on my car phone and the day has started. Because I've laid the groundwork, cultivated the soil, and allowed for rain and sunshine, I can help make good things happen. I begin to anticipate and expect them to happen.

A Self-Starting Company

On a recent airline flight, I was seated next to a woman and her husband. When the conversation turned to what we did for a living, I responded that I was chairman and CEO of The Toro Company. The woman looked rather puzzled. She turned to her husband for enlightenment. "You know," he said, "Toro, the lawn mower company."

I wanted to say, "Yes, we used to be the lawn mower company, but now we're much more." Toro's product range today extends far beyond lawn mowers and even beyond lawn and garden equipment. Our roots date back to 1914, when The Toro Motor Company was founded to build tractor engines for its parent, The Bull Tractor Company. We have long since discontinued producing motors for farm tractors. Our product lines have expanded broadly and have been developed to solve outdoor landscape maintenance problems. People are often surprised to hear that we are the world's leading manufacturer of golf course maintenance equipment and irrigation systems, and that we market probiotic fertilizers, municipal tub grinders, moisture sensors, homeowner composters, turf aerators, landscape accent-lighting, and lake aerifiers. In fact, virtually everything we make and sell—with the possible exception of snowblowers—in some way preserves or enhances the outdoor environment. We have consciously changed our purpose from providing lawn care maintenance products to keeping the world's outdoor green spaces beautiful and healthy.

When I became president, I recognized we would have to redefine the company on several fronts to successfully face the challenges ahead. We needed a vision for the company that directed our resources and strengths toward solutions to outdoor environmental problems. We also needed a focus that would regain market leadership with some built-in flexibility and realism to deal with the cyclical and seasonal nature of our business.

We chose to define ourselves as a self-starting company that keeps the landscape green and clean. We chose to be a company that helps to make the outdoors healthier. We also chose to define ourselves as a company that is sensitive and responsive to environmental issues. The philosophy that led to Toro's new vision came in part from common sense and in part from the belief that you should "view your human environment in terms of your people's strengths."

At Toro we didn't deliberate in lengthy meetings on the issue of making the most of our people resources. When you lose over 50 percent of your salaried employees in one year, "deliberate" isn't the right word. We were *forced* to make the best possible use of our newly founded "bias for action," our inclination, as Nike exhorts, to "just do it." And our people were anxious to contribute and get started on the arduous road to recovery.

Looking for the Opportunities in Adversity

During the recession periods of the early eighties and nineties, there were few people who were looking for good things to happen. I'd often tell Toro employees, "If we were self-starters, we could better control our destiny here. Sure, the environment's tough, and the news isn't always good, but we've done it before. We can do it again."

I had this in mind when the top one hundred managers of Toro gathered together to begin some recession planning in late 1991. I told them, "We know we're in a recession, but I can think of at least eighteen benefits of our being in a recession. Here's what we can do to take advantage of this economic situation." My goal was to help our managers think about the opportunities we could create together. We discussed the tendency of selling systems to slow down in a recession, not only physically but also attitudinally, which gives rise to a self-fulfilling prophecy. Dealers, retailers, and distributors all think, "It will be harder to sell what I did last year because I'll have fewer customers; I'll have to cut my margins to those who do buy in order to be competitive; and I don't want to buy more product from my suppliers because I have too much inventory as it is." This means our salespeople are out on the road, calling on customers who are full of gloom and doom. Writing orders is the last thing on the customers' minds. Well, the best thing a dealer or distributor can have is something new and exciting to sell. The old stuff is boring, more of the same. It just reminds people that times are tough. Often they want to ship the inventory back.

Tough times can actually provide an opportunity to build sales excitement and sell our newer, more innovative products. During the recession, we introduced an exclusive Recycler lawn mower and a unique, water-pulsating greens aerator that really caught the attention of our customers. These were products the competition couldn't offer. New products are something different to talk about and create traffic-building events at the point of sale; they bring life back into your customers.

When you look for opportunities in the face of adversity, you say to yourself, "Yes, we're facing a layoff, that's reality, but what are the benefits of working with a smaller staff?" The answer forces you to prioritize. It encourages you to leverage, or take advantage of the interdependency of your organization or group. It leads you to make quicker decisions about what can and can't be done. You become more efficient and precise, more clear in what you want and in your communications.

This is the time to analyze your work and determine what's truly essential. Anything that's nonessential goes. There's bound to be some waste that has built up over time. Find 5 percent to cut in your department; if you can eliminate 10 percent, you're that much further ahead. Employees who have to take on new tasks because of staff reductions will need to learn new skills. With management's full and enthusiastic assistance, these employees face growth opportunities that will open new doors for them. One role of the leader is to make sure people are prepared to step through those doors.

Switching jobs is one way to prepare people for change. It proved to be a valuable experience for many Toro employees. Here's an account that illustrates some of the benefits to the company and to the employee's own sense of contribution.

> HAVE YOU HEARD the expression, "Don't criticize until you've walked a mile in the person's shoes"? Some Toro employees discovered what it's like to work in another area of the Irrigation Division's plant when a couple of departments started exchanging two employees at a time to experience job demands on the opposite side of their own work cells. Juana Alvarez, a general assembler, and Lucy Juarez, a molding machine operator, were among the first. Before working on the molding machine, Juana wondered why some parts kept coming back with defects. Lucy would say, "There's a lot of pressure in molding. We're expected to do a lot, and we try very hard." Juana learned that most problems are not the operator's fault, that the machines cause difficulties. Lucy said, "We get frustrated when we don't send good parts to the line." Juana could see that the operators wanted to do their best, but they needed more help with the machines from technicians. Lucy concluded: "Everyone should try exchanging jobs. We try very hard to send parts right. We don't want to see that part back again! We want to send it out perfect. Let's catch the problem here before it goes to assembly. We care about the product."
>
> —Karen Bradford

Exchanging jobs gave Lucy and Juana the chance to gain some new perspective, develop their understanding of teamwork, and perform with increased self-confidence and higher expectations—qualities essential to a flexible workforce. Success requires everyone's help and understanding, and when the organization comes together as a team, great things can happen.

During the 1980s, adversity also forced us to develop the habit of thinking like a team. We learned to think in terms of the department, the division, and the company. Reprioritizing and making decisions together brought us through the recession poised, trim, and in good condition to deal with the opportunities of economic recovery. It took three years of struggle and hardship, but we made it through tough times as one big team. And the bonus was we were stronger than before because Team Toro learned to look at challenges as opportunities.

Start Smart

Self-starting, of course, is key to overcoming obstacles and moving your people toward opportunities with the right attitude. But when you're facing constant change, it's just as important to start smart. What's the sense in starting your engine (or your organization) if you don't know where you're going? You may be a prompt and reliable self-starter, but how many times have you charged ahead only to learn you were moving in the wrong direction or weren't sure of what direction you were headed?

Starting smart means you start off together as a team with the right vision. As a manager, you make sure everyone knows the goal. You make sure everyone gets off on the right foot and in the right direction, and that expectations and responsibilities are well defined. It's your role to clearly delineate accountability. And it's your role to see that rewards and consequences are understood by all those involved.

I have a passion for white-water rafting. Some of my coworkers might say that it's a compulsion or an addiction! White-water rafting can be safe and leisurely, accompanied by some fishing and wildlife watching. It can also be a very dangerous and exciting sport.

Today, I have my own tiny armada of rafts and kayaks. Each summer, I lead a group down one of the white-water rivers in the West—the Colorado, the Salmon, or the Snake—or perhaps the Gauley River in the East. We're not as good as the professional guides, but doing it ourselves—relying on our propensity to self-start—creates more excitement and anxiety, which is part of the fun. We also spend a lot of time preparing, educating ourselves, and training so that we can start smart.

With a few early "close calls," I learned that the smart thing to do is to study the river conditions thoroughly, ask the professionals for advice, and scout the major rapids before starting down them. I walk down the riverbank with the captains of the other boats and try to pick out the most difficult areas of the rapids. The roar of the rapids makes it difficult to talk. I need to shout to be heard over them.

On one such scouting run, I yelled to the captains of the other rafts, "See that rock on the left? We should approach it on the right and then point the bows of the boats away from the rock, pulling across the channel, so we use the flow to avoid the hole behind the rock." By planning first we were starting smart, or so I thought. What I didn't know was that one of the captains couldn't hear me and also couldn't discern the river flow from the upstream pouring into the hole. With the water pounding against the rocks all around us, he could only see my mouth moving. When we went down the river, he went down on the wrong side. Why? Because he didn't hear me. His boat grazed the rock, rolled out into the hole, and nearly capsized. That trip taught me a few things. I learned a lot about scouting the rapids you expect to encounter along your path. I also learned about assumptions.

At about this same time, we had made plans to bring all the Toro distributors together to explain our distribution vision. Before doing that, as a check point, we met with six key distributors in Chicago to run through the vision. It was like scouting the rapids while we still had choices and flexibility; we would have time to fine-tune the plan before introducing it to the larger group.

The six distributors listened, commented, and generally supported the vision. After our meeting, I asked each of them to write down the vision as they understood it and send it to me. I wanted to find out if we were all starting smart—to be sure we were starting out together with the same vision. What I got back was surprising. Some of the distributors heard different things, and in general there were gaps in their understanding. I realized that we needed to communicate more clearly, repetitively, and in their language. I learned again that getting everyone together, laying out the plan, and communicating expectations don't necessarily mean you're all starting out together.

When we presented our vision at the general distributor meeting following "the scouting," we modified it to more clearly show a win-win scenario. We took more time to explain it and allowed some questions and discussion time to encourage the distributors to buy into the plan. It was not an easy plan for them to embrace, but most distributors came aboard.

If you believe that your team is together and understands your vision, here's a reality test: Ask your people to describe your expectations or goals in their own words. Have them send you a written response. Analyze their responses. If they can answer your questions the way you would, your team is made up of smart starters. If not, you have the opportunity and responsibility to refocus by clearly resetting the direction and rearticulating the goals.

The attitude you want to instill in your team is that each person has a vital contribution to make and needs to make it. When everyone contributes and values the contributions of others, a team interdependency and bond develop and create a strong momentum that carries the team through normal upsets and obstacles. In today's changing and competitive world, companies require team players who are smart self-starters; otherwise, the enterprise will be disadvantaged in the marketplace.

To define yourself as a smart self-starter, you have to examine your personal and professional strengths, as well as the strengths of your team members. Then you have to put those strengths to the best possible use in your company's environment. This requires discipline and character. Character can be defined as "training created by adversity." In other words, you learn what you have to do to be successful by experiencing hardship. If you want to be a successful team player, you have to be proactive. If you want to be responsible and accountable, you have to be a prime mover and an initiator. In short, you have to be an adventurer.

The Ulysses Factor

One's propensity for adventuring is often called the "Ulysses Factor," designated from the adventures of Ulysses in Homer's epic, *The Odyssey.* People with a high Ulysses Factor have a well-developed sense of adventure. They try to push boundaries out and find new paradigms. Some may consider them reckless, but I would argue that unless we're willing to risk a little, there won't be much achievement.

In our culture, we place a high value on responsibility and accountability. However, the environments we build often curtail people's willingness to take reasonable risks or to try something new. Such climates may encourage people to sidestep or deflect responsibility when things go awry. When people avoid risks and are reluctant to be held accountable, the organization cannot progress. Growth requires some folks who can move beyond normal boundaries to pioneer new initiatives and create new ideas.

I've discovered in myself, and in other achievers, an inclination to step out of our current comfort zones. We have a desire to grow by pushing ourselves to our limits and occasionally living on the edge. Responsibility can't be ignored. You don't take risks unless you accept responsibility; part of leadership means being accountable. Most leaders, however, have a high sense of adventure. They want to push the envelope, to stretch the organization's capacity. My Ulysses Factor has been tempered by some close calls on white-water rafting trips, but I still have a need to confront life aggressively and try new things. This is illustrated by my tendency to push the company harder than it may want to go, beyond its comfort zone. But if Toro is to be a leader, then we must push ahead, past the rest of the pack.

Some people say that I don't have a realistic sense of the organization's capability. They say we can't do all the things I'd like us to be doing at any one time. Not surprisingly, I disagree. I believe we find and develop the needed strength by pushing beyond our current comfort levels. Most of us, in fact, underestimate our capacity to achieve, reach goals, and overcome obstacles. I believe most people in an organization can and will give 110 percent to move the company ahead, to keep it growing and successful, but only if management provides a healthy, nurturing environment that gives value back to the employees. Many people are willing to risk what they have for something better. Of course, they have to have a sense of ownership for what they do and its outcome.

The concept of "owning" your job, or taking pride in it, isn't new. As businessmen and women, it's sometimes difficult to know exactly what we own in our jobs when we don't see the finished product of our work. The intrinsic satisfactions of a completed job aren't readily available because most of us don't produce a product we can see and touch—or we're mired in ruts and routines, devoid of risk and reward.

Overcoming this alienation requires some of the adventuring, accountability, and risk taking that successful leaders and self-starters seem to have. Self-starters can lead a team to anticipate events and conditions that aren't apparent. If you have self-starters on the team, you'll have less waste and redundancy in the system, and the team will be more prevention-oriented. In these terms, self-starting is perhaps the most basic form of leadership. It's being ready and capable of starting at the right signal, the first time. It's being prepared for the effort required of you. It's having your eyes on the prize, right from the start.

Take Advantage of the Multiplier Effect

You're driving down the highway on your way to work. Someone cuts in front of you into your lane, which makes you mad. To get away from this lane jockey, you cut into someone else's lane. Naturally, you make that person mad. Thinking you're a real jerk, he swerves into the next lane. Pretty soon there are countless people coming into work, every one of them ready to start their day angry and upset. Some will take their frustration out on the product or the customer. Others may bark orders at their secretaries and staff. The multiplier effect has begun and just keeps on going.

If you can help someone get off to a good start, however, maybe catch him or her doing something right, it will create a positive effect that can also multiply. Many small, simple but positive things managers, supervisors, and associates do generate momentum that eventually can lead to great things. If you're not too big for small things, you won't then be too small for the big things that might happen as a result.

At Toro we try to take advantage of the multiplier effect by recognizing employees for their small successes as well as their big ones. This is mostly done informally, on the spot, as part of everyone's daily work life. But we also do it formally on occasion. One way we celebrate the successes of the company is "Owners Day." Originally called "Job Holders Day," and then "Employee Day," it began as an annual event to update our people on the state of the company. Now it's a day to recognize and honor the people whose daily personal investments make The Toro Company what it is. We do this with skits, presentations, display booths, and awards. We want our employees to know that small things are important and add up to a healthy company.

As each of us faces an uncertain future, we must realize that it isn't enough to be an observer of change. Part of being a smart self-starter is being an initiator of change. It's our responsibility to take control of our own destiny and future. It is also our privilege and opportunity, for the more we assume and believe in our future's prospects, the more possibilities we will uncover. We must be proactive, anticipate the future, take some risks, be aggressive, and get an early start. Ask yourself if you are growing in proportion to the opportunities before you. Don't let yourself be encumbered by the boundaries of the past.

A leader who is both self-reliant and a self-starter can say, "I'm ready for new things. I'm ready to change and grow." It means you're independent as an individual and interdependent as a team member. When the task requires independent action, you are your own backup team. Keep in mind the words of Karen Clark, author of *Grow Deep, Not Just Tall*: "Change is not merely necessary for life. Life *is* change. Growth is optional."

Leaders are self-starters. And the best leaders are smart starters. They create plans and set them in motion. They understand why they have chosen a particular course. They value feeling good about the course they've chosen. Smart self-starters embrace both thought and action. They are both dreamers and doers.

CHAPTER THREE

Creating a Culture
for Growth

It's not that easy bein' green,
having to spend each day the color of the leaves;...

— FIRST LINE OF SONG "BEIN' GREEN"
SUNG BY KERMIT THE FROG

EVERY ORGANIZATION HAS its own unique culture built on its beliefs and values. Culture is what determines a company's attitudes, environment, and personality. If you work for Disney, for example, you discover the corporate culture is seasoned with heavy doses of "pixie dust," defined as communicating and caring. It's one of the ways Disney people build and maintain relationships. If you've ever been to Disneyland or Disney World, you've seen pixie dust at work.

Some cultures facilitate healthy processes, invigorate the human spirit, and promote proactive collaboration. Other cultures weaken the company's competitive potential and its ability to grow, as well as the individual's sense of well-being. In either case, cultures often develop haphazardly. A choice few are carefully guided and nurtured toward a planned value system. Cultivating a culture is like nurturing a plant—it requires the dedicated attention of a master gardener.

Redefining the Corporate Culture

Like most companies that survived the 1970s and 1980s, our culture at Toro was dominated by a growth and profit mentality. Employee concerns and the processes used to achieve goals were much less important than bottom-line results. "Get the results any way you can, but get the results," was the employees' interpretation of management directives. Such a culture drove Toro for a dozen years or more.

We were caught up in the "big is better" syndrome. We let ourselves believe in growth for growth's sake, and everything that went along with it. We were a company that was both top heavy and bottom heavy. We were a corporate bureaucracy, distant from our employees and unnecessarily formal with our customers. We tried to buy productivity and speed by adding staff at every turn, at the expense of product quality and customer satisfaction. Despite all this, our annual financial reports were impressive—which meant that to the employees, and even to the visionaries and skeptics, there was no reason to apply the brakes.

But when the brakes were applied *for* us by Mother Nature and the economy, we found ourselves needing to redefine our corporate focus, values, and beliefs in terms of absolute standards, such as "back to basics" and "focus on strengths," rather than relative ones. Our goal was survival, pure and simple. Our methodology was to reduce expenses—anywhere. We wanted to renew our emphasis on quality and product excellence. We committed to the development of new products in our core lines. We aggressively drove down abnormally high field inventories. We made frequent, informal, and responsive communications with our customers a top priority. Customer satisfaction, realism, and consistency became our guiding principles. And fostering an environment of employee-driven austerity became essential in managing our costs and expenses.

Creating and building a culture begin with a philosophy. My personal philosophy for success in business is this: Everyone has the potential to contribute to achieving the goals of the company. If you can unleash that potential, market leadership and financial success will be natural by-products. And while it's important to articulate a guiding business philosophy, it's even more important to translate that philosophy into consistent, visible action that is practiced by all, especially the leaders.

And yet, despite the strong support of our entire employee force, the word that best defined our corporate culture was "anxious." We simply had to get beyond the survival period before we could expect any evidence of a servant-leadership environment or empowerment characteristics such as trust, innovation, and compassion.

We wanted our culture to reflect our beliefs:

- What people do and how they feel about it are key to the company's success.

- Each individual has potential. The leader's role is to create an environment where employees can reach their potential.

- An environment of trust leads to more risk taking, innovation, and creativity.

- Empowering individuals and teams to solve problems produces better solutions.

- Increased self-worth will be reflected in greater productivity.

- If a culture values employees, customers, and performance, then quality, productivity, and profits will likely come as natural by-products.

As new management, we wanted to create a winning team. We wanted our team to work effectively and be up to speed regardless of the conditions we faced. Naturally, once economic conditions stabilized, we hoped to face a field that was green and growing. So we began to shape our culture for greener pastures. We adopted a natural process, knowing it would take a long time to complete. We selected the "soil" that would be best for growing our customers. We chose to put principles in place that would allow us to keep things "clean and green." We began working toward the development of a culture that included:

- a mission of sustainable economic growth,
- a selective business focus,
- continued emphasis on product excellence,
- investment in innovation,
- specific people and performance values,
- employee commitment to the company, and
- a strong team mentality.

The results were not only survival and recovery, but a period of unprecedented growth and consecutive earnings improvement based on a drastic cultural change. Once survival and recovery were assured, we introduced a new culture to our entire employee group. That culture is known today as "Pride In Excellence," or PIE for short.

Pride In Excellence

The purpose of Pride In Excellence is to give everyone a piece of the "PIE," to create a work environment that best realizes the company's goals and the goals of individuals, and to steward the assets of the organization. Pride In Excellence describes a culture based on mutual respect and recognition of the worth of each employee. This has evolved over the years to become a combination of six people-values and six performance-values. These blend to direct us to do the right things right, and embody a quality culture that prizes both results and relationships, products and processes—quality in what we do and in how we do it.

The six people-values are:

- Trust and respect for one another
- Teamwork and win-win partnerships
- Giving power away

- Coaching and serving
- Overtly recognizing small success and good tries
- Open, honest, clear communication

These values are based on the guiding principle of genuinely valuing others out of respect and care for their well-being.

The six performance values are:

- Conformance to requirements and standards
- Customer responsiveness
- Sustainable growth and profit imperatives
- Preventing waste by anticipating outcomes and focusing on continuous improvement
- Adding value through innovation and quality in product and process
- Bias for action

Both the people values and the performance values were identified by the management group, about seventy officers and director-level managers, working in large group meetings and small *ad hoc* teams to develop our new culture over a six-month period. One early catalyst was the book *In Search of Excellence* by Tom Peters and Bob Waterman. We selected four of their eight characteristics of successful companies as guideposts:

- bias for action,
- autonomy and entrepreneurship,
- staying close to the customer, and
- productivity through people.

These helped shape the six performance-values now embodied in Pride In Excellence. We illustrate our culture and its relationship to our vision as follows:

Pride in Excellence

People Values		Performance Values		Toro Vision
• Respect & Trust • Teamwork & Partnership • Empowerment • Coaching • Recognition • Communication	**+**	• Conformance to requirements • Customer Responsive • Building Growth & Profitability • Prevention • Adding Value • Bias for Action	**=**	• Purpose • Values & Beliefs • Mission • Vivid Description

We knew that excellence wouldn't come easily. We knew also that if we were to achieve excellence, we could only do so through an environment of mutual respect, trust, and integrity. We would need the open participation of all those involved in setting goals and objectives. And that meant lots of informal and open communication in all directions. Moreover, part of that communication had to be frequent recognition of meaningful performance for everyone.

Pride In Excellence was initiated and fashioned by our entire management team and was communicated to the Toro organization through meetings, activities, printed materials, and by "walking the talk." We knew it wouldn't be enough to present these changes as a program, just as it isn't enough to scatter seeds on unprepared or shallow ground. Our initial PIE activities were the first seeds of a fruitful and supportive culture. We wanted to develop a corporate culture that would provide a climate for individual and company growth. Pride In Excellence is a process, like growth, that is always in motion and always changing. Maintenance of a climate for growth requires continuous attention and action. As actions build on one another in a natural progression, the climate for growth can become self-renewing.

We knew it wouldn't be sufficient to have a few key people in the company stand up and proclaim: "From now on, this is the way we are going to operate." We wanted Pride In Excellence to become integrated into a life-changing reality. We wanted it to be internalized by the workers on the production lines and in our offices as well as by the executives. We were beginning the process of deliberate planting in prepared soil. We were lucky, too, because we could build Pride In Excellence on a strong tradition of employee pride and commitment.

To build our Pride In Excellence culture, we began to create an environment valuing personal growth for all. Pride In Excellence encouraged managers to give employees more responsibility in the decision-making process. Besides encouraging employees to solve problems that can best be solved in their own team environment, the manager's job became to help employees realize their potential, to recognize the contributions of every individual, and to treat team members as if they already were what they were capable of being. This built feelings of worth in each individual and allowed employees to develop feelings of ownership and accountability for their own destiny, become more proactive for the company, and thereby experience the ownership of a shared vision. Employees also had a chance to move from "serving time" in the plant or the office to growing and developing in proportion to the opportunity before them.

Building Pride In Excellence was an ambitious goal. To achieve a satisfactory level of success, many elements had to flourish. From the outset, we accepted that we wouldn't score well for the first few years. We knew that a vision involving trust, humility, and sacrifice would have to allow for failure, setbacks, and only partial or tentative buy-in during the early years. Success, after all, is usually obtained by willingness to risk failure and perseverance in the face of difficulty. People must be free to make mistakes—and learn from them. If leaders both challenge and support their people, those people will often rise to a leader's high expectations, and everyone's self-confidence and self-respect will increase.

PIE in the Sky?

At first, some folks at Toro thought Pride In Excellence was nothing more than "PIE in the sky." I learned that we had to clearly define what Pride In Excellence was and what it wasn't. PIE had lofty goals, but it was a down-to-earth practice. We wanted PIE to be a workable, real-life, real-world undertaking—a foundation on which our employees could operate every day, a solid framework within which they could cultivate honorable business values and personal behaviors. As the following story illustrates, it wasn't easy.

TESTING THE PIE culture by taking a calculated risk was easier said than done. In the early days of PIE, no one believed it was really okay to take a risk and fail, even if your intent was to improve something. It wasn't felt by most employees to be real until one Employee Day when a Toro design engineer, who had tried and failed, was recognized. In conversations people said, "Not only does he still work here, but management actually appreciated his effort and recognized it as a success."

Likewise, the idea that people were now to look for opportunities to recognize others for a job well done was far more difficult to practice than anyone could have envisioned. We were not skilled at it. We were much better at identifying problems and placing blame when something didn't go right.

In my role as participative management administrator, I taught a training course that asked the question "Why?" to get to the root cause of a problem. At first, this was a major culture shock for both the individual asking and the individual being asked. But over time PIE became fun, and most people had fun with it.

—Jim Willis

As Jim points out, we had to show employees that we were serious. To help employees see where we were going and make a commitment to change, we decided to articulate a vision to all stakeholders. By articulating a vision, we hoped to connect everyone in the organization. We wanted to communicate the vision clearly so that each stakeholder could verbalize it, internalize it, and translate it into his or her responsibility. Knowing that people need to see how their work contributes to the vision and mission of the company, we involved employees in forming our "PIE beliefs."

None of these beliefs was formed independently from the others. For example, trusting and caring go hand in hand. They lead naturally to valuing people. You value people as individuals of worth and potential when you recognize their results and reinforce how these contribute to the company's goals. When valuing others becomes part of your being, you can routinely focus on results while maintaining positive relationships at the same time. You give power away so that work can be done more effectively. You see the worth of teamwork and service. You willingly take risks because you trust the power and intent of the support. You know that failure is only a setback—not the guillotine.

As we expected, Pride In Excellence didn't become the Toro culture overnight. Few members of the management team embraced it wholeheartedly from the start; many paid it only lip service. Some thought it wouldn't work because it sounded soft and didn't seem results-oriented. Many saw no need for change. Some thought it would get in the way of sales and production quotas, financial targets, and other bottom-line goals. Others felt it was a threat to their authority and sense of control.

My first task was to get the top management team to buy into PIE. If it was to become a way of life at Toro, they would need to lead. I expected them not only to embrace and espouse the values of PIE, but also to visibly live them as their own. Some immediately did as asked. Even so, they found it difficult to cultivate the culture within their groups and still keep focused on achieving our business goals. They simply couldn't see how to do seemingly contradictory things at the same time.

As we enlisted more managers in the task of creating the PIE culture, we came to expect each other to practice the principles every day. Some learned by example, some were coached by others, and some required outside help to modify their behaviors and style. Still, it wasn't easy. Even those who could see the potential of PIE and who bought in found it difficult to actively support the culture and still maintain a focus on our business goals.

Now, a decade later, our managers know what is required of them. Most managers worked hard to realign their management style with our cultural values, but not all of our managers succeeded. After helping them make some noble attempts to change certain behaviors, we compassionately directed a few people out of the company. Those who have remained have accepted the PIE culture as Toro's way of life. Some lead with a style that is consistent with PIE philosophy; others have difficulty putting it into practice, but they are working at it and making progress. It's a long, arduous process to change the paradigm that contributed to their past successes.

As the leader, I try to recognize progress, even if it's slow. I believe that people want to contribute their best and share the responsibility for creating a quality product or process. For example, most of my employee meetings that update the team on our financial results include a portion devoted to success stories; even small successes indicate progress, and respect and recognition are among the best rewards you can give.

Many employees are reengineering their own work processes out of recognition that we must be competitive. Jim Seifert, assistant general counsel at Toro, tells how he and his team found new ways to think about a challenge resulting in a handsome payoff for Toro.

> IMAGINE THAT TORO is your company. You own it and you are responsible for your own survival. In other words, you are responsible for making a profit. As the owner, you know there are domestic and foreign competitors who want your markets and your customers, and who are willing to work extremely hard to obtain both. My suggestion is that if each of us viewed ourselves as the owner of Toro, we would see more clearly what we need to do in our individual jobs. More importantly, we would work passionately to eliminate waste.
>
> When I came to Toro in May of 1990, I was given the goal of doing whatever was necessary to reduce the company's product liability risk and costs associated with product liability, including attorneys' fees and insurance premiums. I approached the problem as if I were the sole owner of Toro. I asked myself, "What are the

root causes of product liability risk? How does an insurance company view Toro's product liability risk? How does Toro defend itself? What processes are effective?"

After gathering information, the product liability team devised and executed a strategy designed to lower costs and long-term product liability risk. By July 1991, we had achieved results far beyond expectations. Because of our processes oriented toward preventing unnecessary costs, we were able to renegotiate our insurance contract, saving Toro $4.8 million, all because we used the total quality system to reengineer our work processes. No capital investment was needed; no jobs were eliminated; no additional costs were incurred. We simply thought about ourselves, our jobs, and our goals in a radically different way. Some examples are: we organized all work and decisions around reducing costs and reducing risks, which means we now do only work that is either required or makes a difference; we put decision making in the hands of those who have the most information to make a decision; we began using computers to accomplish a goal, not to do unnecessary work faster; we changed our work processes to reflect our respect for coworkers; we emphasized communication—telling those affected what we were going to do differently and why; and we acted as owners by embracing what is important about our jobs—executing our jobs with excellence—and letting go of everything else.

—Jim Seifert

That's the kind of innovation and improvement that comes when people work in a culture that values quality performance and quality people!

Giving Power Away

If you want to make executives anxious, start talking about "pushing power down" or "giving power away." Even if they accept the premise, they have a tough time practicing it on the job. In order to live by our principles and make the PIE culture work, however, we had to push power down and give power away. How do you give power away? This is not something we typically learn to do. It goes against the grain of our competitive upbringing. Actually, it is a subtle process that takes some rather obvious and simple steps.

For example, you can begin by involving employees in setting goals. Initially, this means giving them information. Employees have to be informed of company goals and be made aware of the company mission. You'd probably be surprised at the number of people working for your company who don't even know you have a mission statement, much less are able to recite it. Giving information is inclusion; it invites people in. Informed individuals are more likely to feel a part of things. Another way to move power down is to create problem-solving teams at various levels in the organization and give them increasingly greater responsibility. Soon these teams can become a part of setting goals and strategies.

By including and informing others, you set the stage for four leadership imperatives:

- building trust through openness;

- fostering risk taking, innovation, and creativity;

- practicing a coaching and serving role; and

- creating win-win situations.

These four imperatives are the groundwork for creating an environment for personal growth. In such an environment, you value the worth and contributions of others. You build trust through open and honest communication. You become receptive and learn from those you coach. You build ownership of responsibility. You find ways to encourage, recognize, and reinforce. You freely give both positive and negative feedback in ways that teach and don't tear down another's self-esteem or self-worth.

For example, once four Toro employees—Al, Mel, Dan, and Ray—thought they could save the company time and money using a new method to make the metal hood for our commercial Reelmaster 216 riding lawn mower. Since they represented the functions of purchasing, advance manufacturing, engineering, and design, they were confident that they had considered all of the engineering, materials, and production issues that could upset a smooth completion of the project.

They worked for many months from conception through pilot production, but in the end they found that the new fiberglass technology did not provide consistent quality levels at high manufacturing rates. Unfortunately, they learned this only after it had been implemented during the normal production process—well after the product had been introduced to the field and annual stock orders had been taken. They had invested untold hours in the pilot stages and were certain of its success, but unfortunately, the new process had to be scrapped.

A few months later, I called all four of them into my office. As they gathered outside my office, they became very apprehensive. While their project was long over, the sting of defeat remained with them. As they entered my office, they fully expected to be handed the proverbial "pink slips."

They were completely taken aback when I greeted them with crepe paper, balloons, and refreshments. When I told them it was time for a celebration, they were dumbfounded. I explained that since most innovative ideas don't work out, you need many tries to get a few successes, and that means you need inventors and innovators to keep creating even in the aftermath of failure. The company has to foster a "freedom-to-fail" environment. If you shoot down the teams whose ideas don't pan out, fewer and fewer new ideas will be advanced.

At Toro, we value risk taking because it's an important part of encouraging innovation and self-development. A certain amount of failure is built into the system, so rather than shoot down the attempts that fail, we try to celebrate them. The most important message for Al, Mel, Dan, and Ray was to go back as a team and try something new again. As a postscript to this story, and as is often the case, we were able to use their creative molding process later to assess the effectiveness of future designs.

This was an example of a cross-functional team gelling as they learned together. Initially, it seemed that the application failure had been a waste of time and resources. The experience was valuable, however, and the team's work eventually was significant. Ultimately, it was a growth experience for all of us and an example of our culture fostering the potential value that existed in the initial effort.

The celebration in my office may seem like small recognition for their efforts. It was an easy way of appreciating them and saying thank you. But as it turned out, it had great impact. The story of that celebration spread like wildfire throughout the company. There we were, celebrating the fact that they had invested time and effort in something that failed. From my perspective, these people had invested in us and we were going to invest in them too.

At Toro, in addition to rewarding innovators, we try to recognize and reward everyone who contributes significantly to our success. For example, we have a computer-driven golf course irrigation system called the Network 8000. More than an irrigation system, it's a water conserver. It has built-in sensors that communicate back to the central controller to sprinkle the grass only when needed. As a result, cities and golf courses that invest in it save money. The product has strengthened Toro's market share and has prompted new, related sales.

We celebrated the Network 8000 when we knew the product was a success—when it had an impact on the market and the sales folks were achieving their objectives. We gave our highest award, however, the Circle of Excellence Eagle (an acronym for Employees Achieving Great Levels of Excellence) not just to the sales team but to everyone involved in the project: the engineering project development team, the R&D people, the marketing team, and those involved from manufacturing and control.

This is a perfect example of what can be achieved in a culture that enables individuals and teams to reach their potential. In a trusting environment, everyone is more willing to take some risks and freer to be innovative and creative. People invest themselves more in their work. They work harder—for themselves and for the others involved. A climate of continuous innovation and creative problem solving is a climate for growth.

Innovation Results from Teamwork

People tend to think of innovation as spontaneous revelation grasped by a single person, as when Archimedes exclaimed, "Eureka!" (I have found it!) upon discovering a method to determine the purity of gold. We imagine Thomas Edison at his lab table in the early morning hours inventing by himself. More often, however, innovation results from idea association, idea building, and idea refining when several individuals are working together.

I view our organization as a cluster of teams. Because innovation is an important performance value at Toro, teamwork is fostered and new ideas are valued. When one new idea or perspective is allowed to germinate, or at least is not immediately killed, it often leads to another new idea. In my experience, innovation resulting from teamwork has a much better chance for success. In fact, I have found that the success of a new idea or concept is inversely proportional to the degree of separation between the idea "proposer" and the idea "disposer." For example, marketing often creates strategies and programs for the sales department to implement. If they involve the sales people in the development of the ideas, however, the sales effort will be far more effective.

All corporations are clusters of teams. Many companies are now experiencing success with cellularized and self-directed teams. Good teamwork uses individual strengths to achieve synergy and the whole becomes greater than the sum of its parts. But even after achieving effective teamwork, success may not be immediate. For a team to work well together, the cultural elements of trust, respect, participation, and commitment must be in place. These conditions allow team members to have confidence in one another and to work wholeheartedly toward team goals.

If the cultural "soil" is suboptimal, the team members will work suboptimally. Team members need to recognize the potential for continuous, incremental improvement, even as the team becomes effective. They need to accept change as a necessary and inevitable condition of competitiveness. Constant upheaval is a consequence of an ever-changing market. Team members need to accept and approach change proactively to stay ahead. Once they reach one goal, they must begin to pursue a higher goal. Such continuous improvement is necessary to remain competitive.

Once you give away power to your teams, they'll create more innovation than you ever could by yourself. They will also adopt ownership, trust, accountability, and new idea building. Your role as a team leader is to get the members to adequately prepare themselves and to be smart self-starters. Teach them not just to target goals but also to stay on target. If you help them to focus on the process to continuously improve it, as well as on the results, you will prepare them for more effective work ahead. Well-trained individuals on self-directed teams will enable the company to solve ever bigger problems. As the teams succeed, the company will also succeed, and the company's success will become everyone's success.

Seed Not Sod

NOT ONE BLADE of grass! At least it seemed that way to Lee Albert Durr. His new house was complete. And it was beautiful. The builders had done a commendable job of grading and contouring the surrounding grounds, but only a few trees remained and there was no yard left—not one blade of grass.

Should he go for the quick, easy turf—laying sod, creating an instant lawn? Or should he instead take the longer path, take the time and effort to establish a stronger, healthier lawn by seeding? Either way, Lee knew that all the rocks, fallen tree limbs, and other debris would have to be removed. He had already tested the soil; he knew what starter nutrients and soil amendments to add. The next step was the decision—to seed or to sod.

With seed, he would apply preemergence materials to eliminate the encroachment of weeds, mixed thoroughly with topsoil and fertilizers and hand raked into the yard. Then he would spread the seed uniformly so that every area would have ample opportunity to "bear fruit." More than sod, seed would require measured daily watering to keep the seeds moist until germination but not wash them away as they were taking root.

The decision was his, but for Lee it was not too difficult. He was committed to building a lawn that would endure the stress of long, hot summers and come through the freeze of winter, healthy, strong, and lush. He would seed, not sod.

After the leader has prepared the basis for leadership with a philosophy and sound principles, and has aligned his or her management's orientation to these principles, then comes the building of a vision, culture, and values that provide the footings for the organization's work. A vision is essential for the organization to focus on a direction and destination, as well as a purpose in its work. A culture then provides the "how" of "what gets done." Finally, the values shape the "how" and define the character of the organization.

These endeavors take time to develop. Time is also needed for the organization to embrace the vision and to work congruently within the culture. It will be even more time before positive results surface from the leader's efforts. Nonetheless, vision, culture, and values are essential building blocks to create an environment that will yield long-term corporate growth as well as provide personal growth for each employee. In this section, we explore the ground rules that govern growth, how growth can and must be nurtured, and how to use "the accelerating cycle of success" to gain and keep momentum.

CHAPTER FOUR

Ground Rules
for Growth

*Coming together is a beginning; keeping together
is progress; working together is success.*
— HENRY FORD

ONCE THE MAJOR earth moving is done, we plant seeds in the soil
hoping these will eventually bear fruit for the harvest. We must
observe certain ground rules, however, if we expect to sustain real
growth.

Ground Rule One:
Seed Not Sod

Do we go for the quick fix or for building a good foundation
slowly? Do we lay sod or do we plant seed to get growth? In a culture
that's accustomed to quick results, "seed not sod" isn't an easy choice.
Seeding takes time and quite a bit of care. Eventually, however, it
results in a healthy and more resistant turf.

Each time we faced a crisis at Toro, we faced the choice of seed versus sod. And each time, the choice to seed new growth was difficult to make. When people both inside and outside the company were clamoring for an easy out and a quick turnaround, it was hard to maintain our commitment to a long-range seeding process. More often than not, the hardest task was to keep people faithful to the seeding process when they were saying to themselves, "Gee, if we had sodded this field, we could have been playing ball by now!"

We chose seed over sod because we never believed the destiny of Toro lay solely with the weather, or Mother Nature, or the banking community, or any combination of outside forces. I believed we controlled our own destiny, even though this was very unclear in the early days. I believed our future ultimately lay with the men and women of Toro. With hard work and dedication, I knew we could make Toro whole again. The need for change was there, and in choosing seed over sod, we were opting for grassroots improvement and change.

When seeding for new growth, you must be patient. When you plant a lawn with seed, you don't see much growth for the first few days and weeks. That's why many people are into sod; they like instant results. The question becomes: How do you maintain the faith with those people? How do you keep people from becoming impatient early in the change or growth process, when there are no perceptible improvements or differences?

When I became Toro's president in 1981, the organization, the financial community, and our distributors all wanted a quick fix. They wanted to lay sod. Management, however, didn't see how to do that without sacrificing some longer-term benefits for our people and the company. We could have achieved profitability faster by cutting some important long-term projects in information systems or new product development, but these were needed to regain our competitive edge in the future. Or we could have continued to sell to the mass merchandisers and allowed our service-dealer network to further erode. Instead, we convinced the board, the banks, and the distributors that the best course of action was to "seed the ground" and "cultivate the roots," knowing recovery would take a lot longer.

One breakthrough came after the last workforce reduction had been completed. We gathered all the office employees together in the largest movie theater in town. Steve Keating—former chairman of the board of Honeywell, long-time Toro board member, and chairman of our board's executive committee—joined me on the stage to talk directly and candidly to all the employees. I winced somewhat as I explained, "The person in our organization who is most at fault for where we are today, the person who is most responsible for getting us into this whole mess, is standing in front of you today."

There were others involved. The whole management team shoulders some of the responsibility. But the fact that others, particularly those who had left the company, had caused the ground beneath us to erode was irrelevant. That day in 1981, I had to establish personal credibility with the employees and with other stakeholders such as the banks and the distributors. I had to say, "We're to blame; we've let you down; we've mismanaged the company."

Steve Keating spoke for the board of directors. Steve was a great father figure—a savvy and sage business executive. As chairman of the board he helped Toro with tough banking negotiations, raising $140 million from the banks, even after three of our banks with long-term relationships with us (one spanning forty-seven years) took their money and bolted. With the help of the banks remaining, especially First Bank Systems, and some new ones, such as Manufacturers Hanover, we put together a banking consortium that saved Toro. They accepted our argument against the quick-fix approach and provided the necessary $140 million of working capital to guarantee we would have the resources needed to "seed" a new reality.

At that time the Japanese company, Honda, was emerging as a key competitor. Honda's success in other established industries was frightening. This new competition was fortunate for us, in a sense, because Honda represented a competitor who would invest for the long term—a "seed" competitor not a "sod" competitor. Honda's view of the long term is more like 250 years; they like 50-year plans. They were beating America at the manufacturing game by applying basic principles and fundamental processes, blocking and tackling their competitors, steadily picking at their competitors' weaknesses. We told the banks and others: "Honda is a new and fearsome competitor. They're here to stay, and over time they'll capture market share with fundamental marketing, product superiority, and disciplined business skills. If we try for a quick fix and stop spending money in R&D and engineering, we might recover the ground we've lost, but thereafter we'll be positioned at a competitive disadvantage to Honda. If we stop advertising to get a better profit yield this coming year, and stop investing in the brand name, Honda could replace Toro as the number one name in lawn and garden equipment. If we don't take the time now to rebuild our service-dealer network, Toro's future will be compromised. We might show a quick recovery, but in three years Honda and other Japanese firms will have developed such a momentum that we won't be able to compete against them."

In a very real way Honda was our wake-up call. If our competition had been Snapper, Lawn-Boy, or another American company, our response might not have been as compelling. An American competitor would have been seen as a "sod" competitor and less of a threat to us. But many American manufacturers were learning to fear the Japanese. We were certainly in awe of the Honda presence and were convinced that "quick-fix" approaches wouldn't work against it.

The greatest service the Toro leadership performed at that time was to pull everyone together for a long-term, difficult battle and establish credibility with our constituents and dealers. To do that, we had to be up front about what we were and weren't going to do. We told the banks and our employees, "It's going to take a long time for us to recover. We might lose money for awhile, but we're going to report to you every month on our progress against a well-detailed plan." And we did exactly what we said we were going to do; we delivered the numbers.

We gave the banks a detailed pro forma each month so they could keep a constant tab on our progress. Since our credibility, as well as our line of credit, was at stake, it was important to deliver on our commitments. The master credit agreement we signed was restrictive and expensive, but it was the only way we could get the capital we needed to compete and stay in business. Previously, Toro had overpromised and underdelivered, and the banks were especially cynical about our new management team. We had to impose a discipline on ourselves that the company had lacked in the past. It was difficult to deliver on our short-term goals and still be building for the future with some long-term initiatives, but that's the challenge of real leadership—and it is a common challenge in today's business environment.

The single most difficult step we faced was paring down from 4,100 employees to about 1,800. To this day I hate the thought that we had become so excessive that over half our workforce lost their jobs. Our leaner group was left with just one goal—survival. Because we all had the same agenda and we were faced with a crisis, it was relatively easy to develop a team mentality. The discipline and focus we'd lacked when we were more bureaucratic came more easily under crisis conditions. Of course, it's always simpler when you don't have any options.

The metaphor of seeding not sodding is useful to illustrate the importance of long-term solutions, difficult as they are when they put short-term goals at risk. The unfortunate reality of it is that the short and long run often compete and we are usually predisposed to take the quicker approach. Hopefully, competitors like the Japanese and also our customers are convincing us otherwise.

Ground Rule Two:
The Team Comes First

This concept can be hard to accept initially because there is a bit of the maverick in most of us, which the American culture celebrates. As a result, we have a high propensity to honor individual heroes. We celebrate men and women such as Neil Armstrong, Norm Schwartzkoff, Colin Powell, and Christa McAuliffe—we often think of them as if they were solo heroes. We think differently, however, when we consider the masses of technicians, engineers, and unnamed individuals who stand with them and make their accomplishments possible. Many heroes are just the most visible members of impressive team efforts. Without each member of the team aimed in the same direction and sharing the same mission, their individual heroism probably wouldn't have been possible.

At Toro, teams are about building a more open and involved organization. We've built a strong team mentality by demonstrating the value of self-direction, empowerment, cross-functioning, and synergy. The organization has responded with a tremendous use of teams for solving problems and creating opportunities. Our employees are teaming in a cooperative spirit that permits every member to grow and develop personally and professionally in a culture that enhances opportunities for corporate success.

One leadership task is to view the team members in terms of their human strengths. Our role is to enable and empower team members to use their strengths. They can then more fully accomplish work that is satisfying and meaningful to them, which benefits both the team and the company.

Ground Rule Three:
Provide Guidelines and Support

Before you will see much growth, you have to provide people with guidance and support, especially if the concept of teamwork is new to them. Many managers put a team in place and then discover the people are not empowered to run a project. Like the old horse that pulled the milk wagon a few generations ago, your team may only know one way of working—and the fault is no one's but your own.

At Toro we struggled to develop teamwork and its synergistic value during our growing years. We still struggle with this because of emerging ideas and concepts such as paradigm shifts, employee involvement, personal empowerment, self-directed and cross-functional work teams, and job ownership. These ideas have helped us view teamwork differently, and the more we have learned about teamwork, the more encouraged we have been that we can make it work.

We drafted the following affirmation, included in our vision statement:

> Our employees will know that their work and efforts are vital and significant to the company's success. We will encourage and support professional growth and help each employee achieve his or her highest potential. The result will benefit our customers as well as our employees. The primary focus and reason for being here will be to satisfy the needs of our customers as well as encouraging and helping each employee to reach his or her potential.

I have found that Stephen Covey's books, *The Seven Habits of Highly Effective People* and *Principle-Centered Leadership,* offer the best framework for building team synergy and individual stewardship. Covey suggests that to achieve synergy, we must be centered on principles and processes, not policies and practices. By being principle-centered, team members avoid the turf battles that are common in organizations.

Five guidelines make up Covey's "win-win performance agreement" and what he calls "stewardship delegation," that is, the delegation of resources and responsibilities to individuals. His guidelines establish a clear, up-front, mutual understanding of mission, roles, and goals. They also clarify expectations.

1. *Specify the quantity and quality of the desired results.* This starts you with the "end in mind," and requires you to prioritize the important tasks (put first things first). You can also develop milestones and timetables, along with ways to evaluate progress and outcomes. Remember, what gets measured gets managed.

2. *Specify the guidelines (the boundaries and parameters) of the job.* Here you can determine the work domain, and just as importantly where and what to avoid pursuing. This helps you create a road map toward the desired end.

3. *List all available resources.* Identify your available human, financial, and physical resources. If you don't know exactly what's available, you may overlook the key to success. Remember to view your human resources in terms of their strengths. Let that knowledge allow you to allow your people to do their best work.

4. *Define responsibility and accountability.* Schedule accountability progress reports. Specify performance criteria. The old saying, "A day late and a dollar short," was meant for just this principle. Timeliness and performance criteria have to be clearly defined and understood by everyone involved.

5. *Describe the consequences and rewards.* State both the positive rewards of success and the negative consequences of failure. Let consequences reflect the natural result of the actions taken.

My commitment to these guidelines comes from a growing awareness that it isn't enough for leaders to read the right books and attend the latest seminars. It doesn't matter how well intentioned your efforts may be. What is needed is commitment to and bone-deep belief in the process and the people on the team. You have to produce genuine concurrence within the day-to-day working environment between what is said, what is done, and how and why it is done. At Toro, I learned you had to create an environment for individual and team success. I learned that the goals of management and the goals of the employees who dedicate their time to the company aren't so far apart. I learned these goals are mutually attainable. In fact, they'll either be achieved together—or not at all.

Ground Rule Four:
Close the Perception Gap

One exercise I use with my managers points out the gap between management's and employees' views of what creates job satisfaction. Managers are asked to rank ten job satisfaction factors *from the employee's point of view.* They rank the most important factor to the least important factor from the following set of job satisfaction factors:

- Feeling of "being in" on things
- Interesting work
- Full appreciation of work done
- Job security
- Good pay
- Loyalty to employees
- Good working conditions
- Promotion and growth
- Help with personal problems
- Tactful discipline

Later, I reveal a comparison of how a group of managers thought employees would rank these factors to how the employees themselves ranked them. The results are usually surprising:

Managers' Perceptions of Ranking	Ranking by Employees
1. Good pay	1. Interesting work
2. Job security	2. Full appreciation of work done
3. Promotion and growth	3. Feeling of "being in" on things
4. Good working conditions	4. Job security
5. Interesting work	5. Good pay
6. Tactful discipline	6. Promotion and growth
7. Loyalty to employees	7. Good working conditions
8. Full appreciation of work done	8. Loyalty to employees
9. Help with personal problems	9. Help with personal problems
10. Feeling of "being in" on things	10. Tactful discipline

—K. Kovach (*Advanced Management* magazine, 1985)

The two lists indicate a significant management perception gap. Many managers believe their subordinates would be satisfied to stay at any job as long as the pay is good and the employment is secure, without regard to the top three factors on the employee ranking. Even if these employees were satisfied as such, one would have to question their contribution and level of quality over the long term in this environment. Moreover, how secure can people feel if a company doesn't care about its people? Executives who believe recognition and appreciation are unimportant are missing a vital piece in employee relations. Genuine expressions of appreciation contribute significantly to employees' ongoing willingness to make the contributions necessary for personal and corporate success. In addition, it seems to follow that if a manager wants to nurture and improve people's opinions of themselves, he or she must recognize the positive contributions they make.

I believe these misconceptions exist largely because we're locked into old ideas and norms. We all have concepts of what the words *management* and *labor* mean. We see them as two distinct and separate things. For the twenty-first century, more accurate and more positive terms would be *team leaders* and *team members*.

Ground Rule Five:
Select Team Members

How do you create teams? You first build a team out of your resource pool, taking into consideration the diversity and talents of the group. But it's also important to insure that the different personalities and styles blend. Doing an audit of the group using the Myers-Briggs profile is a useful way to look at individual members of a team. Another method is CARE, which stands for Creator, Advancer, Refiner, and Executor—the four dominant attributes that author Allen Fahden concludes contribute to each person's innovative make-up. CARE evaluates each individual's propensity to participate in the creative and problem-solving process. Fahden's book, *Innovation on Demand,* makes a strong case for balance on the team so that you have strength represented for each phase of the problem-solving process. For example, if your team is comprised of nothing but creators and executors, there will be too many failures due to a lack of understanding between the two types.

We incorporate three basic premises in the selection method we use at Toro: (1) each one of us has great potential; (2) potential is best achieved when people are allowed to perform; and (3) the best performance comes from people who are inspired, motivated, and encouraged; committed to a vision, goal, or task; empowered to execute their vision; and recognized for their part in completing the vision.

Ground Rule Six:
Empower the Team Leaders and Members

Once the team is selected, empower the team by clarifying expectations, goals, schedules, parameters, roles, responsibilities, consequences, and guidelines. Empower team members by allowing them self-direction and freedom to fail. A leader's role is to create an environment where people can achieve their potential as they move toward their goals.

Team building is like a home-improvement project—it isn't accomplished overnight. It's a matter of creating interdependency, a win-win mind-set, and a commitment to the team and its goals. It involves planning, tooling, training, measuring, building, and finishing. The men and women I talk to when I visit Toro's outlying locations understand that management's job is to deliver, among other things, an acceptable profit and financial return for The Toro Company. Our employee-shareholders know that my role as CEO is to grow green grass in fertile soil. I have chosen to grow green grass by leading a team to achieve our mutual goals. I want to inspire not rule or control, to build trust not fear or insecurity. I want to lead by winning support not by creating opposition, and to be trustworthy not manipulative. This is my vision of a leader.

Remember the film *Star Wars*? Near the end of the story, the rebel pilots are trying to hit a tiny target on the massive Death Star.

They're outgunned and facing massive odds. The one constant in the background is the team leader's voice. Sure and steady, he tells them, "Stay on target; stay on target; stay on target." It's a vivid illustration of leadership. Likewise, every team leader needs to keep team members focused on the target and let them exercise an appropriate degree of initiative and creativity in the methods used to get the job done.

For many employees, our Pride In Excellence (PIE) philosophy initiated their first experience with empowered teamwork on the job. And for many, like operations manager Jim Willis, it came as a bit of a surprise.

> IN GENERAL, for most plant employees, PIE and participative management were synonymous. It didn't really affect them other than every so often the "big" guys would show up and hand out PIE. For what reason, no one was quite sure. I think most employees were looking for a PIE cookbook. Instead, it was as though we were given the theme and told to write the script. In retrospect, that was probably the only way it could have been done.
>
> —Jim Willis

I agree. Empowerment doesn't mean giving people all the details of how to reach the goals. It means allowing the team the freedom to find the best way to proceed.

Unfortunately for many, the metaphor of "serving time on an assembly line" comes very close to the truth. By the mere act of passing through the gates of a manufacturing plant or doors of an office building, they're transformed from a position of individual, self-empowered greatness to a "Captain, may I?" existence. Why does this happen? These are the men and women who face the same routines day after day. They can be simultaneously grateful for and resentful of their nine-to-five existence. Getting them to commit to a vision, goal, or task can be a challenge.

I'm not a romantic with a skewed view of reality. I just believe it doesn't have to be this way. I believe that the company and its people can benefit mutually and expand their horizons in ways that, before making the effort, they hardly dreamed possible. My position permits me to share this vision with other people and to help them make it a reality. In order to be sustained, however, that reality has to be held by all involved.

Ground Rule Seven:
Kill the Seeds of Discontent

When I'm in small groups, I frequently talk about empowerment, valuing differences, respect, involvement, and the freedom to control your own destiny—goals that we, as Toro management, have targeted. Often employees are skeptical. Sometimes our behavior conflicts with our talk. It's management's job to demonstrate commitment to the core values and beliefs. Each of us must visibly and proactively "walk the talk."

Often skepticism and cynicism fester within the supervisory ranks. This can be very confusing to employees: to hear one set of values and have quite another imposed within their work environment. This incongruence sows the seeds of discontent; it also creates the perception of management disharmony or lack of integrity, and undermines the very vision and culture we are entrusted to nurture.

Such a dichotomy between what is said and what is done tears down team building, much like a dull lawn mower blade damages grass. You suspect the destructive elements are there, but unless you examine the turf closely, you don't know for sure. You may not have noticed, but a clean, sharp blade on a mower cuts right through a clump of grass. It gives you a true cut that results in a healthier lawn. A dull blade bends the grass and tears it. If it does cut the grass off, the edges will be torn and ragged. Five days later, the grass will be brown, having been bruised by the dull blade. A few days later, the grass blades may be dead. Do that over and over again, and you create an environment for fungus and disease. The grass won't be green and healthy. Fungus and disease can set into teams and organizations, too. Employee "brown out" and "burnout" are the fruits of discontent. To avoid such diseases, you must either sharpen the blade or replace it. Managers and leaders can't be vague or communicate mixed messages to the team. Their blades of behavior must be sharply consistent with what they preach.

At Toro we also try to insure that our managers recognize seeding opportunities and nurturing situations. For example, recently we developed an aggressive commercial fertilizer program that entailed a new natural fertilizer with some unique performance characteristics combined with an integrated sales and service support system for the distributor. Implementation of this program meant a sizable investment by the distributor. It included purchase of a sophisticated device to analyze soil and tissue samples, as well as a commitment to hire a turf specialist whose responsibility would be focused totally on the fertilizer business.

We intended to introduce this campaign to distributors in high-potential markets only, recognizing that the other distributors would be less apt to make the investment. Our director of marketing, however, felt that we should help distributors in low-potential markets by testing a couple of their golf courses where the application might be directed at a specific problem on selected tees or greens. We wanted each distributor to have a test result in his market covering a couple of years, so that when we rolled out the program, he would have a golf course superintendent or two who would act as opinion leaders to validate the fertilizer claims and support the business opportunity. This would give those distributors a jump start and a sense of confidence to go forward using selected golf course superintendents as key sales people in the process. This was a "seeding process" that the management team wanted to initiate so that the program would be sprouting when we were ready to introduce it in low-potential markets.

I have the power and responsibility as CEO to require that Toro managers be committed to our vision, goals, and projects. This is a big and challenging assignment. Our employees judge our leadership integrity by our behaviors not by our intentions. Generally speaking, our managers need to be genuinely committed to the principles we espouse. I want them to believe in and care about unleashing individual potential. I want them to understand that the best performance comes from people who are inspired, motivated, recognized, and encouraged. As leaders, our job is to enable our teams to fulfill the corporate vision, and to recognize the achievements of each of our teams.

Several managers had problems with this team philosophy. In the United States, we are brought up on individual drive. Our culture is full of stories of the poor or disadvantaged individual who makes it on his or her own with entrepreneurship and ambition. I understand this, and I understand the managers who say to me, "But Ken, I am where I am *because* of my individual drive. I wouldn't be here if I weren't willing to take risks—to go it alone and rise above the crowd. If I hadn't been ambitious and met the challenges, I would never have made it this far." These are the ego elements that make up a dynamic management talent. I tell them, though, that we have to start giving up our egos by pushing the power down, letting go of the control, and becoming coaches. Management consultant Ken Blanchard defines ego as "edging God out." He says that ego addiction is the main cause of management failure because it causes people in management positions to suppose they really know all, to hoard power, and to destroy trust.

When we push power down through the organization, our people begin to rise to their potential and trust the environment to support them. Trust is our reward, and it's an essential element in building teams and in reaching goals. When you give up ego power and all its trappings, you get back trust. Trust may be the toughest element to attain and maintain in an organization, but it's worth the effort. When you have trust, a certain magic begins to happen.

Ground Rule Eight:
Do Unto Others

No one knows more about creating magic than the Disney organization. Michael Eisner, Disney's chairman and CEO, expressed it well when he said, "If you take care of your people, the dollars will take care of themselves." Disneyland and Disney World are in the magic business. Their philosophy about their "cast members" (what Disney calls the employees) is this: "Cast members are treated as we expect them to treat Guests (spelled with a capital G). If we treat our people properly, they will treat our Guests properly. We motivate our cast members not by promotions or threats, but by caring."

The leader's role is to create an environment where people can achieve their potential as they move toward their goals and work to help us achieve ours. At Toro we ask our employees to make a commitment to whatever corporate or division entity they work for. We expect them to do their very best work as individuals and as team members. In return, we work to help them meet their goals with the understanding that we win or lose as a team.

For example, when employees in the Irrigation Division recognized the need to improve our product development process, they formed a committee and went to work.

A CRITICAL LOOK at the Irrigation Division showed an inability to get products to market on time and within budget. As a result, Toro was losing market share and sales. So we formed a new Product Development Process Steering Committee to create a process that would make us more competitive. This was a great leap forward for us because our products must work, they must be on time, and we must make a profit. The goal of excellence in product development became a shared responsibility. To achieve that goal we improved the communication processes among customers, suppliers, and staff; we improved product cycle times, operating margins, and customer satisfaction by establishing benchmarks and measurable improvements in each product line; we set clear-cut guidelines that outline authority, responsibility, and role definitions; we trained team members to become team players, knowledge resources, customer advocates, problem solvers, and decision makers with visibility throughout the division.

Our mission statement was to create an environment for product development that utilizes cross-functional involvement and results in the highest quality products developed in the shortest time frame that meets or exceeds customer requirements and the financial goals of Toro.

Steering committee members devoted about five hundred hours per person to this cause. I was pleased to participate on this team because team members were very professional and able to debate issues without bruising feelings.

—Greg Kliner

Toro's long-term financial goal is to be a company that can demonstrate consistent revenue growth and earnings performance in the face of our inherent seasonal and cyclical vulnerabilities. We build a platform from which to pursue this goal by being trustworthy and valuing associates and our team members. That leads to a more productive and contributing organization. Then when everyone is directed to satisfy customer requirements, market leadership becomes more likely. Market leadership, in turn, enables consistent and sustainable growth in earnings, a target that attracts and holds shareholders.

Toro's philosophy is depicted in the following triangle, the descriptive symbol of Pride In Excellence. The vision we have for our company is contained in a positive feedback system that works like

The Toro Philosophy

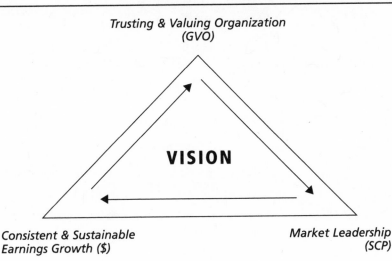

Trusting & Valuing Organization
(GVO)

VISION

Consistent & Sustainable
Earnings Growth ($)

Market Leadership
(SCP)

this: When you have a trusting and valuing organization, that is people who genuinely value others (GVO), you enhance the ability and drive of the organization to satisfy customers, thereby building market leadership, or at least strengthening your competitive position (SCP). As the company's competitive position strengthens, its growth in revenues and earnings is positively influenced. Financial health that is consistent and sustainable creates the capacity to invest in the organization's well-being and thereby its environment for personal growth. This, then, further enhances competitive position and subsequently earnings growth.

Our team members, our people, therefore, are our most important assets. We believe it; we say it; we live by it. What they do and how they feel are key. Their willingness to risk and their dedication to continuous improvement combine to make us successful. These are the ground rules for growth. These are the critical factors for continued growth and prosperity today and into the next century.

CHAPTER FIVE

Nurturing Growth

Growth is the only evidence of life.
— CARDINAL JOHN HENRY NEWMAN

WHEN THE NEW SHOOTS of a plant push above ground, giving first evidence of life, we know two things: the roots have taken hold below the ground, and the young plant has a long way to go to reach maturity. As I think of our attempts at cultural change in this context, I see several parallels. Before new shoots begin to show above ground, the foundations of cultural change must root themselves into properly prepared soil, and the right seeds have to receive sunshine, water, nutrients, and shade. Only then will cultural change emerge in the anticipated patterns and shape.

And while this emergence of cultural change may be cause to celebrate, it is important to remember that, like the young plant, the new culture is extremely fragile and can be easily uprooted. It needs to be carefully nurtured. A management support system is needed, not only to foster the culture but also to prevent backsliding to old ways that could damage the new growth.

Management Support Systems

Wise leaders give followers the support they require in early growth and development stages to enable them to internalize changes. Support systems nurture a positive climate for young sprouts that aren't strong enough to stand upright on their own. The leader's job is to make sure the environment is the best it can be—to encourage a fast start and a strong finish for everyone. After a while, employees will catch the spirit of this and support each other! How can leaders create such a supportive environment? I see four ways:

1. *Vision.* As it states in Proverbs: "Where there is no vision, the people perish." Unless people buy into the vision with a sense of ownership and learn to act in ways that support and sustain the vision, it will be little more than a far-out dream that dissipates over time. The leader must insure that the team understands the vision and starts off together, or they may end up pursuing different goals.

2. *Motivation.* A leader who initiates cultural change with a vision, but fails to enroll and motivate his/her team plus build a structure for proper support, is like a baker who prepares the cake mix in the pan, places the pan in the oven, but never turns on the heat. The leader's job is to make sure that the oven is on, that there is an incubating environment for the culture to grow, and that people are warmed up.

3. *Communication.* Like a cake, a culture can't rise without leaven. Leaders supply leaven by communicating their vision so that others in the organization can understand it and translate it to their work lives. The leader is responsible that everyone knows, understands, and embraces the vision. Leaders clarify expectations, define responsibilities, and make sure all involved understand the rewards and consequences.

4. *Participation.* Although our vision and mission at Toro were instituted through a top-down process, the changes we put in place could never have taken root had they not been internalized by our employees. The potential for apathy and recalcitrance, even sabotage, exists in all organizations, and it can be silent or difficult to discern. You can minimize this potential by encouraging everyone to participate in the company's journey, to feel part of its "family," which is a powerful and gratifying experience. Participation comes easily in a nurturing and supportive environment. We encourage activities that give people a sense of family and participation, whether it's aerobics classes or Toastmaster meetings in the cafeteria, personal development and health-related activities, athletic teams such as golf and softball, or even choral groups, drill teams, and personal support partners.

One employee who became involved in a support group affirms that the spirit of community is alive and well at Toro.

WHEN I WAS ASKED if I would be interested in joining a support group, I quickly replied, "I'd love to." How relieved I felt. The many demands on my life weren't allowing me the time I needed for the social and spiritual growth I wanted. By the end of our second meeting, we had created a vision and mission statement and established guidelines and strategies for our group.

After six months, our group has grown. Through word of mouth we are receiving many requests, and new members are coming to our meetings. We have a phone list that all members can use to send messages and requests between our meetings. We are supported and thanked by many for our stewardship and efforts. Our foundation has been established and our seeds sown. We will continue to harvest and show others we care.

—Pattie Murphy Bukowski

Pattie's support group reflects an environment of community and family, but the support group is not directly supporting the goals of the company. Can such an environment develop and grow around company issues? I think so. Employees grow and bond in an environment of processes and practices that involve them in the company. Remember the perception gap we discussed in the last chapter? The top three employee preferences were *interesting work, full appreciation of work done,* and *a feeling of "being in" on things.* People like to feel included. They like to understand where the company is going and what its goals are. They appreciate hearing progress reports and knowing results. If we share information openly and frequently with our people, they are more readily enlisted in achieving excellence today and tomorrow.

In another study, conducted by Lou Harris in the late 1980s, 74 percent of the employees surveyed rated "making a contribution" as important to them; 82 percent of the employees rated "challenge in the job" as being important; and 71 percent said "deciding how to do their work" was important to them. At Toro we have consciously tried to provide an environment where people can fulfill these goals. Managers are trained to empower, trust, and coach their people toward more autonomy and ownership. Empowering people to do what they do best does not mean, however, that the supervisory levels can abdicate their responsibility for the performance of their groups. In fact, members of our management group receive financial incentives as part of their annual compensation based on how well they have met their leadership objectives as rated by subordinates and peers. Our managers realize how important it is for them to uphold their responsibilities because they must pass the acid test from those whom they manage.

Greg Kliner, director of operations of our Irrigation Division, tells his experience with Toro's commitment to encouraging our people to decide how to do their work and to feel accountable at the same time.

WHEN I RETURNED to Toro after a five year absence, it was like working for a different company. During those five years, the PIE culture was introduced. Now there is pride in accomplishment, concern for the employee, an emphasis on teamwork, consistent direction from the upper management, and genuine concern for each employee. Decision making has been decentralized, meaning leaders no longer dictate the methods for achieving results. When team members devise their own methods and are successful, the leader shares in the victory. We have an inverted pyramid—the leader serves the people by removing barriers and mentoring. The Chinese philosopher Lao-tzu said a lot about what Toro is trying to become: "A leader is best when people barely know that he exists, not so good when people obey and acclaim him, worse when they despise him. 'Fail to honor people, they fail to honor you'; but of a good leader, who talks little, when his work is done, his aim fulfilled, they will all say, 'We did this ourselves.'"

For example, when it was decided that we would move from a volume-oriented manufacturing process that lacked proper focus on customers, quality, and cost, to a process that was customer focused and quality driven, many people thought it was foolish to suggest such a different approach. I heard all of the reasons why it wouldn't succeed.

Ken Melrose and our management team, however, supported me. Our sense of passion to make a difference was renewed and was supported from the highest levels. I found that the greatest tool I had to work with was the positive attitude of my staff and our hourly employees, who also believed they could make a difference and be a part of the solution, not just the cause of the problem.

The real test came the day it was announced that we were going to absorb manufacturing, engineering, and scheduling into work teams. This plan involved the dissolution of two departments. The announcement rolled through the division like thunder. This was our first step in flattening the organization. I wanted to put the resources where they could have the most impact—in the day-to-day manufacturing operations. Over time, it became apparent that this was the right thing to do. But when we rolled out these new processes, they were not instant successes—productivity dropped, rejection rates went up, and every alarm bell in the division went off. This was merely a part of folks learning a new way of doing their work. Within two weeks, we were right back on line and we've never looked back. We were given the freedom to fail, were supported in our risk taking, and were encouraged to give away power to the functional areas within the organization.

Many companies talk about focused factories, empowerment, team building, and change, but they are not willing to take a chance. At one time, I admit, I was concerned that we were moving too fast. But the support received from senior management gave our team confidence, encouraged us to move forward, and encouraged the functional teams to come up with more ideas for improving product quality and customer focus.

—Greg Kliner

A Leadership Success Model

After reviewing leadership training programs available from outside, we concluded that Toro needed a customized program specific to our culture and our concept of leadership. So we developed a training course for our current and promising leaders that incorporated our PIE values. Virtually all of our management-level people have now completed the course.

Because of my conviction about leadership at Toro and the values of our culture, I wanted to make a personal statement to all of our supervisory people. I figured the best way to do this was to be one of the trainers, so I began teaching the first module to each participant. I started by laying out the philosophical foundation and set of principles from which the leadership concepts evolved. I then presented the cultural elements, the values, and the behaviors that I believed would build and nurture the organization.

This leadership model is based on a simple premise: If the leader focuses on the needs of customers and employees, expects and encourages results through valuing relationships, and recognizes people for their contributions, the likely outcomes will be a greater sense of trust and accountability leading to more risk taking, creativity, and innovation; a stronger team that multiplies its ability to meet customer needs; and greater empowerment to solve problems at grassroots levels leading to better solutions, increased feelings of self-worth, and greater productivity.

Such leadership requires a unique balance. First, you have to be a servant of the organization; you must defer to its potential power, but at the same time, channel its effective use. Second, you have to keep the organization focused on financial goals. You must be careful not to get caught in a "big is better" syndrome or a "growth for growth's sake" mentality; rather, you want to balance growth and financial health with creating an environment that can sustain these year after year. Third, you must weigh what's best for the employees with what's best for the company, and as you do so, be clear and firm. Make the process as important as the end result.

One of leadership's toughest challenges is knowing when to lead by taking charge, when to lead by backing off, and when to lead by giving up control, by empowering your people. I invite you to try this exercise: Think about the word *supervision,* and list the associated words that come to mind. Most of your words will probably have to do with how you characterize the role of management, perhaps in traditional terms. We easily get locked into terms like *subordinate, boss, control, hierarchy, rank and file* because these terms characterize our experience of supervision over the years—the supervisor and the subordinate. But over time our view of supervision is changing.

If you trace the definition of *to boss* from the 1950s through the 1980s, you see an interesting trend: In the 1950s, the definition included phrases like "to ride roughshod over" or "to shove around." In the 1960s, *to boss* would favor "to control, order, or command." In the 1970s, we see some softening of the term—"to guide" and "to direct." In the 1980s, we see the introduction of the concept of "coach" and of a person's ability to develop as "a boss." I predict that sometime in this decade a new meaning of *to boss* will emerge; it will be "to serve and to steward."

While time and the pressures of the marketplace alter our practices, views, and motivations, a new perspective can also reorient us. Try making a slight change in the word *supervision* and notice the difference it makes in your word association list. Take the word *SuperVision* and list the words that come to mind. Then compare your two lists.

When I teach our Building Better Leadership Skills course, I divide the class in half and ask one group to list the words that come to mind when they see the word *supervision*. The second group lists the words they associate with *SuperVision*. The differences in their lists are illuminating. Here's a sample of the lists from each group.

Supervision	SuperVision
1. Guide	1. Acquisition
2. Training	2. Successful
3. Direction	3. Future
4. Delegate	4. Foresight
5. Organize	5. Broad View
6. Decision Making	6. Risky
7. Instruction	7. Drastic
8. Motivator	8. Big Picture
9. Teaching (Coach)	9. Total Involvement
10. Coordinator	10. Periscope (Up/Over)
11. Mediator	11. Opportunities
12. Counseling	12. Strategic
13. Quality	13. Dreams
14. Expectations	14. Innovator
15. Feedback	15. 20/20 Eyesight
16. Boss	16. X-Ray Vision
17. Narrow	17. Intuitive
18. Traditional View	18. Passion

As we continue to move our culture forward, the comparisons are less dramatic, but typically the group who sees the word *supervision* still lists words that are more traditional and narrowly focused on the things that supervisors do to people. The other group transcends the boundaries of experience to include more future-oriented perspectives and progressive actions. Very few, if any, words from the latter group's list define the things supervisors do to people. It's an effective exercise because the perception of the word *SuperVision* takes on a new meaning for the participants. Would you rather excel in *Supervision* or *SuperVision?* And would you rather work for a *Supervisor* or a *SuperVisor?*

Seeds Begin to Sprout

After instituting these cultural changes and being challenged to live them every day, we began to see some significant changes both in attitudes and the bottom line. Studies showed that morale improved, as did commitment and teamwork. Productivity jumped. Sales per employee more than quadrupled. Our quality was once again rated the best in the industry. Over a period of a few years, products from our Consumer Division earned nine best buys or number one ratings from leading consumer product magazines; within that same time period, dealers who sold our type of equipment changed their quality impressions of Toro products from mediocre and substandard to the top of the pack.

Moreover, product innovation abounded. We developed and introduced more new products in the period following these cultural changes than in any other five-year period in the company's history. Several of these were major market-share breakers such as:

- high performance, hand-held blowers/vacuums

- power mowers that recycle cut grass

- hydro-injection greens aerators (for decompacting golf course greens with high-pressure water jets)

- walking greens mowers that cut grass to a 3/32 inch height

- five-gang hydraulic fairway mowers (for precision cutting of fairways giving an almost-putting-green appearance)

- electric snow throwers

- water pressure compensating sprinkler heads

- moisture control sensors to regulate watering

- pressure-regulating valves (valves that regulate water pressure)

- curve-chuted rotor snow throwers (snow throwers with advanced throwing capabilities)

- rain switches that automatically prevent sprinklers from running during rainstorms

- golf course irrigation controllers providing two-way, electronic communications between the superintendent's office and satellites out on the course

- wide-area walk mowers for commercial cutters (high capacity estate mowers)

Our culture now stressed ownership by participation, accountability, and empowerment. We wanted all employees to be self-starters, to control their own destinies, and to feel the worth of their abilities and contributions. We wanted everyone to feel ownership of their job and of the corporation's vision, mission, and goals. We knew that if we truly wanted people to take ownership of job responsibilities and the corporate vision, we would need to provide ownership in the company itself. So we added to our profit-sharing plan a ten-year employee stock ownership plan (ESOP) that would make our employees shareholders. With the establishment of an ESOP, employee ownership of the company rose from 4 percent to over 20 percent.

Earnings improved every year from the beginning of the cultural change throughout the eighties, in spite of two snowless winters and the drought of 1988—conditions that almost killed the company in 1981. This was the longest period of uninterrupted earnings growth in our history, and unusual for a company dependent on weather. Wall Street began to value us differently; the stock price rose nearly tenfold over this period—testimony to the importance of sustainable earnings growth to stockholders.

Defining Excellence

Early in our Pride In Excellence development, we felt that *excellence* meant flawless or perfect. As we began to establish standards and goals and experience the process of achieving them, we quickly realized this was unrealistic. Excellence then became a standard of superiority or preeminence; it came to mean "to exceed, to surpass, to be better." We retained the more extreme definition, however, as an attitude for achievement. It parallels the difference in the total quality vernacular between *continuous improvement* and *zero defects.* Setting a goal of zero defects within a given time frame for some objectives can be impractical and demoralizing. On the other hand, continuous improvement can accelerate momentum and enthusiasm within the team as milestones are reached and exceeded. There is, however, virtue in advancing the concept of zero defects or perfection as the ultimate goal. I believe an attitude of moving toward zero defects is important, but employees are most motivated by achieving goals that are both challenging *and* realistic.

A leader who challenges the team to move toward excellence faces a personal challenge—to create and maintain an operating environment that engenders trust and empowers action. This takes time to achieve and is fragile, as a team can easily be destroyed by the absence of management visibly "walking the talk" or by signals and behaviors that are inconsistent with values.

Mel Foss, senior advance engineering buyer, tells the story of how one demonstration is worth a thousand speeches.

IN JULY 1987, I was a senior buyer working in our Materials Control Department. One day I had a meeting with the president and executive vice-president of a major supplier to Toro. We had just entered through the front lobby of our headquarters and walked over sticky wet floors—a consequence of some local flooding that caused significant damage to the entire office facility. The carpet had been removed in an effort to mop up the water and dry things out. I remember that my visitors' comments were unfavorable because of the mess we had to endure. We sat in my office trying to do some business, but the conversation kept coming back to the flood.

Then, outside my office, we heard a ruckus. I started to get up when through the door came this man serving cookies and lemonade. He said, "Good morning," to me and to my guests and asked if we would like some refreshments. We all agreed, and he served us.

After he left the room, the conversation turned from the flood to the surprise service. The visiting president asked, "Who was that person? Does he do this often?" I will never forget his reaction when I told him, "The man who just served us is the head of Toro, Ken Melrose."

He actually choked on his cookie. He couldn't believe it. We started to talk about business philosophy and the leadership principles at Toro. I told him that our CEO really believes that people are the most important assets of the corporation, and that he not only believes this but lives by this standard. In fact, he returned home from a national show to be with us and lift our spirits after the flood.

They were most impressed, and I will never forget the stunned look on their faces as they listened to me. We all took something away from that momentary encounter.

—Mel Foss

Well, Mel, thanks for remembering that. I was glad for the opportunity to be of service—even if it was only to serve refreshments! But more important than the lemonade and cookies was the chance to "walk the talk," to demonstrate commitment to Toro's most valuable asset, our people.

As leaders, we must continually reinforce and retrain management to model our principles and practices. Exactly how difficult this is becomes clear when we remember that the environment should permit employees the "freedom to fail." As I've said before, freedom to fail leads to more risk taking, which results in more innovation and creativity. The organizational culture must also foster empowerment to be more effective in solving problems. Grassroots problem solving has the advantage of viewing the problem from experience at its base level. Your culture should also provide the freedom and encouragement to move toward self-improvement. It should permit people to develop their full potential, which will contribute to their feelings of self-worth and result in personal satisfaction and improved productivity.

If you create a culture in which employees, customers, and performance all are valued and are clearly the important priorities, then quality, productivity, and profits will be natural by-products. You may ask, "But what if I do all these things and the result is unmitigated failure? A culture such as Pride In Excellence sounds great in theory, but I'm the one who answers to senior management. If my team fails, I'm the one who has to pay the piper." That, of course, is often the case. But if you build a strong team and create a productive team environment via selection, training, guidelines, expectations, and a healthy cultural framework, you will create an environment of trust and autonomy. Since you are accountable for the results, performance values must be balanced appropriately with people values to achieve excellence and to avoid having to pay the piper.

Targeting Excellence

Even the best of teams and plans go awry. Knowing that, how can we avoid failure? I recommend the following three practices.

1. Specify the performance values and identify the goals for everyone, including yourself, so that each team member clearly understands the expectations.

2. Appraise the behaviors of team members, including your own, to insure alignment with company values and beliefs.

3. Help team members to establish methods to monitor progress against the goal of "zero defects," 100 percent of the time, in processes as well as results.

This is the principle of conformance to performance values and conformance to people values—results and relationships. This discipline enables the team to best focus on conforming to the requirements of the customer, whether the customer is inside the company or out in the marketplace. Conformance to customer requirements is essential because nonconformance violates expectations and your reason for being: satisfying your customers. One reason why the Taurus development team at Ford was so successful was that each team meeting began with an update from the field or from market research regarding customer requirements. A review of what the customer wanted set the priority and context for all other issues to be resolved.

Make the importance of satisfying the customer crystal clear to every member of your team. Paint the vision at the beginning, insuring that the team understands the goals. Work through the processes that best serve customers, as well as team functions, and the processes that help the team embrace the vision. Make sure the team understands the consequences of not meeting the goals; continually keep the customer requirements current and visible.

Keep in mind that customer requirements and satisfaction are not limited to the initial, or "out of the box" product experience. We know that a customer who is happy with his new Toro lawn mower can easily be turned off by poor service, a restrictive warranty or inflexible policy, or the unavailability of critical parts. So we talk about "total product," which includes all aspects of the product experience with the customer. We must meet the customer's expectations at the first point of contact and at every point of contact thereafter. Remember, you're shooting for excellence and total customer satisfaction.

One of my favorite examples of employee empowerment at Toro comes from one of our loyal lawn and garden dealers for the Consumer Equipment Division. Years ago, Terry McGovern, owner of Arthur's Equipment in the Boston area, was visiting our Windom, Minnesota, lawn mower plant with a group of dealers. As he walked down an assembly line, he noticed one of our employees affixing a hangtag to the recoil starter cord of each lawn mower as it passed her station. He asked her to stop the line so he could tell her that when his sales people try to demonstrate the mower's easy starting feature to prospects, the hangtag inadvertently tears away from the cord. The problem sounded real enough to her, although she had never thought of it before, so she relocated the hangtag on the very next mower. Terry was dumbfounded—instant customer satisfaction by an empowered Toro employee.

In the team environment, encourage open communication in all directions. Get team members involved as much as is feasible. Value their ideas and work with them to glean the goodness of each idea. Orient your people not only toward success, but also toward excellence. In that way, you create a learning environment and you facilitate lessons, experiences, processes, guidelines, and opportunities for improvement. While your role as a leader is to be a coach, your behavior also establishes the team's work ethic; you become the model for the team.

You have to be overtly goal driven at the same time as you are creating team-building processes. That way you can require the same from every member of your team. Commit to unleashing the potential of your people, then find ways to do it. A good coach encourages his team to think for themselves and provides room to try new ideas, but within a defined playing field. As the team project progresses, provide recognition and acknowledge everyone's contributions and achievements. Find ways to encourage your team's continued development and growth. Have the team share the pride in both their personal and group achievements—among themselves as well as with others. Expect team members to achieve their goals and demand the same from yourself. Seek out opportunities to be proactive in eliminating and preventing errors.

Empowering others isn't about abdicating your leadership role. Achieving excellence demands that you help your people develop and grow, and that you improve your own performance of all leadership tasks. By leading, we are inviting others to fashion themselves according to our model of what a leader can and should be. Do this correctly and without reservation, and you'll find yourself working harder than you've ever worked before. You must be willing to confront employees with concerns regarding subpar performances, misunderstandings, conflict issues, and differing points of view that require clear and honest resolution.

All of these activities can be done in a way that respects teams and individuals who are not measuring up. At times, the leader must step in and refocus the team, get the team back on track, and determine what action must be taken. Sometimes the leader may even overrule the team's decisions. The leader is ultimately responsible for both the growth of the team and the results. But by enabling others to accept their own accountability and create their own outcomes, the leader helps individuals to develop an increased capacity for contribution and responsibility and develops his or her own capacity as well.

Recognizing the Experts

At Toro, retaining our employee force is another way of nurturing the culture. If a company experiences a consistently high turnover, someone had better ask why. High turnover means a company is losing both proven and potential talent. It is very expensive in time and effort to constantly train new people, and if you're not building loyalty, then your investment in training is largely wasted. It's hard to build a sense of belonging when turnover is high, and you can't achieve the excellence your company is capable of achieving.

I'm never satisfied with our employee turnover rate even though it is less than half the national average. In fact, many of our former employees return to Toro. They tell us they left because they thought the grass was greener somewhere else, but they return when they learn otherwise. I believe our turnover is low because we focus on what is truly important: moving the power and authority to the people who execute the plans and know what is really needed for our success.

One way we have found to recognize the people at the grassroots level of Toro, the people whose contributions boost productivity and lead to excellence, is a management-plant participation program. All the company officers work one day a year on the assembly line in most plants. We don't expect the officers to actually learn the jobs, but we do expect them to gain a little experience and empathy by walking in another person's shoes.

The first time we tried it, our executives worked the entire day on the line in our Windom, Minnesota, plant where most of our lawn mowers are assembled. By the end of the day, we could assemble mowers at no more than 80 percent of the standard line rate— slower than the normal speed of the conveyor slats at the beginning of each work day. Of course, I'd rather not list all of the quality problems we created. But the plant employees had a great time. We established that their ability to build mowers both quickly and accurately was far superior to ours. It was clear to us who should be making the decisions regarding lawn mower assembly.

The experience turned a group of skeptical employees into a bunch of enthusiastic coworkers. They learned that they could solve their problems better than we (management) could because they were the right people at the right place with the right information. Our job was to create the environment that allowed them to do just that.

After our day at the Windom plant, we decided to do this in every plant. And in every plant, the men and women on the lines proved that they were the experts and we were the apprentices. We have begun learning to let go, to empower and entrust, and to have faith in outcomes when we give up control. That's been difficult for most of us and the process has been slow, but we continue to strive toward the goal.

The Evolution of Culture

Our Pride In Excellence culture continues to evolve. As Publilius Syprus wrote more than two millenniums ago, "It takes a long time to bring excellence to maturity." Organizations are organic; like any organism, they constantly grow and adapt. As Toro's culture evolved during the eighties, we moved from a period of building and nurturing to one of maintaining and sustaining. In this preservation period, we spent time enhancing and enriching the environment we created. As we began the decade of the nineties, however, our world changed again. Another worldwide recession left its mark on Toro.

Depressed sales and earnings were followed by restructuring and reorganization. This, of course, had an impact on our culture. While it was different from the culture challenge ten years earlier, the need for reinvention and rebuilding was obvious. As we moved out of the recession, we began to discover ways to rejuvenate and re-create our environment, and actually used this time to move our PIE culture to the next plateau.

The journey is never over. The changing needs of our people and of the world continue to challenge us to take the next step, to anticipate, to respond to the future with flexibility. As leaders, we must continually cultivate the environment to allow for personal and professional growth because, in the long run, the best way to adapt to the future is to continually grow. We need to actively embody our vision in our daily work. Our people must possess an inner passion that demonstrates sincerity, enthusiasm, focus, and commitment to our core values. People are a company's single most important asset, a company's only real, long-term sustainable edge. In fact, the people *are* the company.

I always try to remember who the real experts are. The numerous contributions individuals make add up to the success of the company. Their productivity, plus their continued well-being, help create the company's continued well-being. The power of problem solving, of continuous improvement, of quality and innovation, of action and reaction, all reside with the people who make the products, deliver the results, and who directly serve internal and external customers. The best culture is one that builds trust, empowers people, and encourages them to create and accept the outcomes. Companies that care about their people, that care about their future, and that nurture an environment for growth deliver the best long-term outcomes.

The goal is to lead and treat your people as an appreciating asset, not only to enhance the current performance of the company but also to build its future. You do this best by investing in your people, by SuperVising them for their own long-term personal growth, well-being, and contribution. Making long-term investments in your people parallels the concept of "seed not sod." It's how we define who and what we are. It's how we define what our values are. It enables us to start smart, to finish strong, and to achieve excellence. In the process, we work to create and sustain an environment of growth in all realms—personal, team, organizational, and corporate.

CHAPTER SIX

The Accelerating Cycle of Success

Evolution is not a force, but a process.
— ANONYMOUS

AUTHOR JAMES MICHENER tells a tale that helps explain what keeps him writing:

WHEN I WAS FIVE, a farmer living at the end of our lane hammered eight nails into the trunk of an aging, unproductive apple tree. That autumn, a miracle happened. The tired old tree produced a bumper crop of juicy red apples. When I asked how this had happened, the farmer explained, "Hammering the rusty nails gave it a shock to remind it that its job is to produce apples." In the 1980s, when I was nearly eighty, I had some nails hammered into my trunk—heart surgery, vertigo, a new left hip—and, like a sensible apple tree, I resolved to resume bearing fruit.

In the early eighties, we at Toro felt the rusty nails that shocked us into a new reality. I remember thinking frequently, "What are we as a company doing? What is driving our actions? How do we know if our strategies will bear fruit? What *are* our fundamental strategies?" It seemed we needed to get back to basics, back to the kind of blocking and tackling that made the company strong in the past, because I knew we could excel there. I knew, too, that if we didn't have strong core businesses, we were certainly risking too much trying to extend ourselves. It made me question whether or not we were on the right track with many of our initiatives.

A period of crisis is often a period of assessment and reevaluation. As we laid the groundwork for seeding a new vision and culture, we learned that new strategies were needed to regain a leadership position in the marketplace. We also realized that those strategies should be offshoots from our vision and our strengths: a dedicated, loyal, and committed workforce; a product-system oriented to innovation and excellent quality; a mentality of high customer satisfaction; a broad, versatile distribution system; an expertise in turf-grass maintenance; and a strong brand-name image. From these strengths come strategic imperatives that are both compatible with our vision and geared toward building and sustaining competitive leadership.

A Single Strategic Imperative

The Toro brand name means many things to people. The words people use most often to describe Toro are innovative, safety conscious, quality, durable, lawn and garden equipment, lawn mowers, reliable, and well-engineered. Toro's products are rarely seen as having the lowest price. Our image implies that our products carry high value-added content. People will pay prices in accordance with the value they receive. That's why we invest heavily in new ideas and provide the support systems to implement them. We also enjoy a reputation for high quality. We continue to aggressively fund comprehensive, continuous improvement efforts, even though we believe quality is mostly a matter of employee attitude and responsibility.

Today's customers expect high quality and are no longer willing to pay a premium for it. We feel our return on quality comes from the lower cost of doing it right the first time. Over time, this has given Toro a strong image in the upscale segment of each market in which we compete. To enhance our reputation, we continue to emphasize innovative products and dedicate ourselves to the strategic imperative of *total product leadership,* as we have throughout our eighty-year history. This fundamental strategy has guided us to create products that deliver high added value through exceptional performance and after-market service. It is the beacon that keeps us on course during good times and bad times.

Total product leadership goes beyond the product itself; it embraces the total customer experience during the product's useful life. It includes the image, positioning, and reputation of the brand that preconditions a customer. It includes the delivery system of that product, which means the interface between the ultimate customer and the seller, whether the seller is a dealer, mass merchant, contractor-installer, or distributor. Total product leadership also includes aftermarket service, which is comprised of parts delivery, repair and maintenance services, and direct customer service with the manufacturer. Customers recognize the "total product" superiority of the Toro brand and are willing to pay for it.

Because of our long-standing dedication to total product leadership, we have a very strong "brand equity" in the name Toro. But we can't stand on reputation alone. We have to both add new and enhance existing products and services that deliver on customer expectations. To do that, we consistently invest in the creative process. Our product development system is oriented to finding product uniqueness that customers will value. We emphasize upgrading old products by incorporating new innovations into them. While we've made research and development an important component in identifying breakthrough ideas that push the current state of a product to a new plateau, we recognize that creative ideas can occur anywhere and germinate best in open, brainstorming teams. Since we focus on ideas that create greater satisfaction and value for the customer, we need constant interface with the customer. Typically, customer-driven innovations command high margins for reinvestment opportunities and strengthen market positions of product leadership.

We've discovered that to sustain total product leadership, we need an environment that allows creativity and risk taking to flourish. Such an environment allows engineering, marketing, sales, and manufacturing people to create new ideas and to take some risks to advance those ideas toward commercialization.

A System That Delivers

Traditionally, our product-to-market flow has been through distributors to dealers who serve the end-user customers. This has worked best for us because a seasonal product that depends on the weather requires a quick-response system to changes in demand. Moreover, a Toro lawn mower typically has features and benefits that need face-to-face salesmanship at the point of sale, so a comprehensive distribution system offering quality presentation is important. Trained representatives demonstrate the product to consumers, showing them the value-added elements that add up to the product being innovative, safety conscious, durable, reliable, and well-engineered—elements that make the product a Toro.

Part of the salesperson's role is to demonstrate to customers that the Toro product is worth the price they pay. This role requires both sales ability and training. It also requires a delivery system that enhances the salesmanship and delivers the service support the product requires. Our service capability depends on a network of servicing dealers and the rapid availability of parts. We also have a communication network that allows us to satisfy customers quickly and comprehensively. In addition, we have in place service training schools and the entire support system implied by all the links in our service chain. We believe this service capability adds to the uniqueness and superiority of our product, contributing to total product leadership.

People don't choose Toro products just because we build good lawn mowers and snow throwers. Many other companies build outdoor equipment. People select Toro because the brand creates high expectations, and the product plus its aftermarket support systems deliver on these expectations. That creates product integrity. This sense of integrity is important because it brings a special "magic" to the Toro brand. The brand has come to stand for confidence, peace of mind, honesty, reliability, and a heritage of individual craftsmanship.

We at Toro carefully nurture this image and are keenly aware of the value it has to the customer. Our strong reputation gives our new products and innovations early acceptance in the marketplace—we can move into new markets with reasonable confidence that customers will welcome products that carry the Toro name.

On the other hand, the preconception consumers have of Toro can inhibit us too. Because we don't want to convey the impression that we also make less expensive, lower-priced products, we can't enter low-priced market segments with much credibility. In some cases, this inhibits our sales potential as well as the points of distribution available to us. We do not, for example, sell very successfully through channels whose primary value to the consumer is low pricing. Such distribution channels exist to bring the customer the lowest price possible in the most efficient manner, and that generally means no individual sales presentations or service support. While this meets the needs of certain customers, it is difficult for us to execute a premium-brand strategy for a complex, service-oriented product in this retail segment; therefore, we carefully position ourselves based on value rather than on price.

Our success has come primarily from products that stand out above the rest and therefore demand attention. Toro products may cost more, but each Toro product offers valuable benefits to the customer—benefits worth paying for. I want every member of the Toro family to understand total product leadership philosophy and its concomitant premium brand strategy. This philosophy and its implications must be shared and embraced by each employee.

Success Means Higher Margins

In the early seventies, Ogilvy and Mather became our advertising agency. Its greatest contribution to Toro over the years has been helping us understand the value of our brand equity, our market strengths and position, and the overall ethos of our company. Ogilvy helped us clarify those elements and protect them as an inviolate principle and Toro's *raison d'être.* This principle came to be called "the accelerating cycle of success," and it is illustrated in the diagram below.

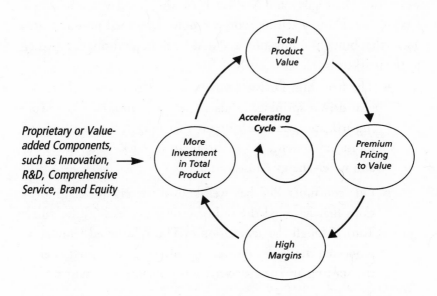

The cycle begins with the development of a product of sufficient distinctiveness to command a premium price which yields a higher margin than its competitors' in the market. This premium price is acceptable to consumers only if the product brings additional value-added benefits. The resulting higher margins then enable the company to aggressively promote and explain the product through advertising, and to deliver and sell the product through a high-quality delivery system. These not only explain the product's benefits, but also build an investment in the brand name and reinforce the image and positioning of the brand as a whole. Furthermore, the margins generate enough of a premium to cover the costs of bringing more new value-added products to the marketplace in the future.

When launched into the marketplace, these future innovative products cause the cycle to be repeated and spread throughout the

company. More innovation creates greater margins for more investment opportunities for even more innovation, while at the same time
the brand continues to strengthen, creating a larger customer following. This accelerating cycle of success had been a predominant,
although implicit, guiding principle for the company even before it
was defined by Ogilvy and Mather. It continues today as one of our
strategic linchpins. Each division can point to several product cate-
gories that brought innovation and new levels of performance quality
to the marketplace:

- The Irrigation Division boasts unique, trendsetting, plastic,
  gear-driven sprinkler heads as well as environmentally leading irrigation control systems that operate on the basis of
  moisture content, evapotranspiration rates, water pressure,
  and water-energy conservation.

- Our consumer line has well-known rotary mower innovations that have led the industry since the early fifties when
  Toro, through the acquisition of The Whirlwind Company,
  pioneered the rotary mower and added features such as electric starting and gear-driven, self-propelling mechanisms.

- Toro has been the leading manufacturer of snow throwers,
  primarily through its superior technology and innovation in
  high-capacity, user-friendly snow-throwing products that
  clean right down to the pavement.

- In the appliance area, over the last ten years, Toro has introduced products such as the electric blower vac with a suction
  rate of 190 miles per hour. In a "face off," the Toro vacuum
  will literally suck all the air out of the competitors' vacuum
  bags, forcing them to collapse.

- Since 1932, Toro has pioneered golf course maintenance
  equipment for fairways, greens, and sand traps. Its worldwide reputation is largely due to innovations in reel and
  rotary grass cutting, as well as new ideas in turf health and
  care.

A story on innovation in the August 1993 issue of *Fortune* magazine featured Toro's HydroJet 3000 greens aerator. Greens suffer from tremendous compaction of the earth because of the constant use they receive. The compacted earth prevents water and nutrients from seeping down to the root structure of the grass. To solve this problem, the ground has to be aerated—loosened in some manner to allow the root systems to breathe and to receive the water and nutrients they require to grow. The traditional way to aerate grass has been to use a device that drives hollow metal tubes four to six inches into the ground and pulls up plugs of turf and grass. These plugs then sit on the greens until they can be swept off. The residue from the process leaves the greens lumpy and stressed for several days, and play is usually held up until the putting surfaces can be returned to their original smoothness.

Instead of using intrusive metal tubes to relieve compaction, the Toro HydroJet shoots high-pressure water jets into the turf, penetrating the ground to a depth of four to six inches as the machine moves across the green. As the water penetrates, the compacted earth is loosened below the surface of the greens, and water and nutrients are able to reach the root systems. With no plugs to be swept off the greens, play can be resumed as soon as the HydroJet moves on.

In the future, devices like the HydroJet will deliver fertilizers and nutrients to the soil in solution with the water, all in one step. This "fertigation" process hasn't been brought to market in a major way yet, but it's only a matter of time before the technology is developed and can be consistently produced.

The accelerating cycle of success is critical for organizations and their people. If we truly believe people are the most important asset of any corporation—more important than brand name, innovative products, or distribution systems—then we must invest in this cycle of success for them as well. It is in the constant, continuous investments in our people that the success cycle grows and expands.

Translating the Vision

To move toward tangible results, an overarching vision must be translated into strategic actions. At Toro that vision has been focused by deploying a creative organization segmented into venture teams with a customer focus in an environment that allows free thinking and risk taking. To help demonstrate what that looks and feels like inside Toro, here are four accounts told by Toro employees.

WHEN THE FIRST PIE TEAM was formed in November 1983, eight members were appointed to represent various areas of the company. We met with Ken Melrose and he explained his vision of the new Toro culture. Along with this new culture came a new language—management by walking around, skunkworks (small, *ad hoc,* focused teams) celebrating successes. Each of us studied the basic concepts of the new culture and what the role of the PIE Team would be. We struggled with how we would introduce this new culture to the employee base. We felt our plans were too complex; we needed to keep things simple. At last the team reached a decision on how to introduce the PIE culture.

The first event would take place on George Washington's birthday. We hung signs that said "PIE IS COMING" all over the building. The day arrived and much to the surprise of the employees, they were served *cherry pie* by the officers. For some time after that experience, a piece of pie became a form of recognition.

We also introduced the employee name badge with the Toro philosophy printed on the reverse side. It begins: "We believe the single most important factor that influences our success as a company is the Toro employee." We rewarded people who wore the name badges. But the new culture seemed to start slowly, leaving us frustrated. We wondered if the management team was merely going through the motions.

Weeks passed and months passed. We were experiencing a change taking place. Some ignored it, others adjusted to it, and a few championed it. As a long-term member of the PIE Team and an advocate of change, I began to see a new culture emerge—a culture where employees valued each other. The employees believed in a vision and became the vision.

On Friday, July 24, 1987, ten inches of rain fell in the Twin City area in one day, and tornadoes did some heavy damage west of the metro area. It was the rainfall of the century. On my drive to the office that morning, I battled the flooded roadways. Some major freeways were impassable, and traffic was tied up. I was thinking, "Since this is Friday and we're on summer hours, this should be a five-hour work day." I arrived late to work that morning, but when the parking lot came into view, I saw that there were only a scattering of vehicles in the lot. I immediately spotted our facilities leader, Bill Hayes, standing outside of the building looking dismayed. I walked up to Bill and asked what was going on. He said that a wall of water had broken through the back of the building, flooding the Parts Department.

The newly constructed Engineering Department, which I am a part of, was located next door to Parts. We had only occupied our new space for a few months. There was still four inches of water on the floor as I sloshed across the new carpet to my office. At this point, I was convinced that it would be several days before we could return to work.

But what took place over the weekend was unbelievable—it was a miracle. Our facilities employees organized a cleanup that would not only remove the water from the building but also remove the ruined carpet. Many key employees worked through the weekend. In Engineering, the computer room floor was underwater, but ComputerVision, our support to our CAD system, flew in from Boston to work with our technical personnel through the weekend. By Monday morning we were fully operational and dry. This could only have happened in this time frame because the people at Toro cared about each other and about the company. Pride In Excellence was at work.

—Mary Miller

ERNIE JOYNER started working for the Toro Company some forty-three years ago; today he exudes the Pride In Excellence philosophy. Even at his age, Ernie still walks three miles to and from work. Until two years ago, he jogged. He has to stay in shape in order to jump—jump 12,000 feet out of an airplane that is. After 335 jumps, Ernie still enjoys his sport. And after forty-three years, he still enjoys his work as a machinist in the Minneapolis plant, producing high-quality parts.

Ernie applies his beliefs about jumping to his work. You only get one chance, so do it right, and most of all, enjoy what you're doing. In forty-three years things changed, and Ernie helped to bring about those changes. A good example occurred recently.

There was a quality issue with a part being made in the Minneapolis plant and assembled in Tomah. Ace troubleshooter Joe Boll had an idea about how to correct the defect, but he needed the input of the local experts to find out if it was feasible. He bounced the idea off engineers Paul Kurth and Mozus Kats, who got Ernie involved. Ernie worked closely with the tool and die men, Bob Fuerstenberg and Bill Erickson, and presto, the problem was solved. It took experts and teamwork to bring about the changes needed to insure our customers receive a quality product at competitive prices. And that's Pride In Excellence.

—Jim Willis

I FOUND A HOME at Toro. There is a magic here that retains your interest and loyalty through ups and downs. My job has become a career because of the Toro culture. It begins with the people Toro hires. It is fostered by the environment in which we work. It is an atmosphere of highly charged idea people with a "can do" attitude. In my sixteen years at Toro, I have worked for most of our senior managers. Every one of them has given me the credit for work done well, and I have felt valued. I have been given visibility and growth beyond anything I imagined when I began work at Toro as a secretary. The environment has propelled me to take on challenges and allowed me into situations that I would not have sought on my own. This has made it possible for me to advance and has given me reason to try harder. Toro let me believe I could make a difference, and I haven't been disappointed.

In this company, everyone is accessible to everyone else. Chain of command is not a barrier to employees in need of answers or direction. It is a company with a community lunchroom where all levels can and do sit together and share meals. It is a company where everyone is on a first-name basis. It is a culture where we are free to voice concerns. We are, for the most part, employees who care so much that we are never satisfied with "good enough." We always believe Toro can be even better.

Toro has a formal name for its culture, Pride In Excellence. It allows people to be recognized publicly for achievements, but greater than that it is not driven from the top down. Everyone is encouraged to nominate a peer, subordinate, or teams for recognition when something distinctive is achieved. Our leadership supports and nourishes this culture. It enables us to become productive contributors by allowing us the freedom to thrive through success and failure.

—Carol Duning

IN MY TWENTY-THREE-YEAR career at Toro, hardly a working day has passed without visitors and vendors calling to offer a new or different product or service. During the first half of my career, I would dutifully escort these visitors to my office and then routinely deposit them back in the lobby when the interview ended. Since the culture changed at Toro, I now take visitors into our cafeteria and hold our discussions there—not to be closer to the coffee urn but to purposely expose our guests to Main Street, the product displays, the historical photographs, the Circle of Excellence Eagle, and the certified vendor plaques.

Upon leaving the cafeteria, I often pause to point out that the offices of our chairman and president are "right over there," not in the usual insulated corner of the building. Not a single transportation supplier has ever seen or heard of such an arrangement.

And I know when they walk down the steps away from Toro they are thinking, "Wow, this place *is* different."

—Keith Clark

As these four accounts so beautifully attest, our culture encourages free thinking and risk taking. There is a freedom-to-fail mentality, with accountability. The foundation, of course, is trust. Without trust, people are reluctant to propose new ideas or to push the organization beyond boundaries never before crossed. They will even be reluctant to advance suggestions that carry small risks. But in many ways, that's what a healthy, growing organization needs to do in order to harvest the best fruit.

Strategic imperatives that emerge as outcroppings of the vision are essential, facilitated by a culture that nurtures and promotes growth. They all build strength and health over time. Fundamental strategies are not short-term ways to exploit opportunity. Strategic imperatives, like vision and culture, take time to grow. After seeding, they need nurturing and support, and need the faith and trust that they will bear good fruit.

Walter Chalmers Smith wrote, "There is no vision but by faith." I learned that developing faith is like planting seeds. Even if some of our seeds fall by the wayside, we will still receive some harvest. Any act of faith will bless us. Indeed, the Toro Team acted on faith as we planted much seed. Slowly, just in spots at first, sprigs of grass sprouted. Then came more. Some didn't make it. But gradually enough took root, and the company had a new foundation—a vision, a culture, and a team ready for growth.

Managing and Maintaining the Turf

AFTER CAREFULLY SELECTING and preparing the farmland for the crops he would raise, and after deciding to "seed not sod" the yard around the farmhouse, Lee Durr was set to begin managing the growth process and maintaining the operation. Both processes required his attention, personal commitment, and his vision of a beautiful outdoors, a clean and green environment.

In the field, he had to decide when to increase and when to limit irrigation. In the yard, he had to determine daily when to water and how much—when to cool the grass to protect it against extreme heat and when to "deep water" the crops to make them more resistant to drought.

As carefully as he had applied the organic fertilizers in both areas, it was still necessary to weed, removing foreign and invasive growth. Cultivation became a constant duty, as did aeration in those areas prone to compaction from heavy use.

But even on days when he was exhausted, Lee knew in his heart it was his daily diligence in nurturing both the field and the lawn that enabled him to joyfully anticipate the harvest.

In many ways, the hardest test of leadership is not building but maintaining the new environment or the plan. Maintenance requires continuing the same work that built the foundation: walking the talk, resisting the quick fix, building trust, and exercising patience, perseverance, and courage. A strong foundation of principles and values is needed to resist the expedient solutions that reflect our myopias and boundaries. Constant nurturing and focus eventually lead the organization to the desired results, but it takes a disciplined leader to stay the course.

As a leader, you must understand the correct use of power, how to serve, and how to build and maintain trust. To insure continued growth, you must be willing to break barriers, conserve and renew resources, actively create your own future, and establish winning strategies.

CHAPTER SEVEN

The Correct Use
of Power

Power tends to corrupt; and absolute power corrupts absolutely.
— LORD ACTON

A FARMER WENT OUT to sow his seed. As he was scattering the seed, some fell along the path, and the birds came and ate it up. Some fell on rocky places where it did not have much soil. It sprang up quickly because the soil was shallow. But when the sun came up, the plants were scorched, and they withered because they had no root. Other seed fell among thorns, which grew up and choked the plants, so that they did not bear grain. Still other seed fell on good soil. It came up, grew, and produced a crop, a hundred times more than was sown.

This parable from the New Testament, told almost two thousand years ago, contains much wisdom for growing corporate cultures today. At Toro, the sustainable initiatives such as total quality, core business processes, and our PIE culture are crafted not hurriedly, but carefully and comprehensively. We want to be certain the right seeds are sown in good soil and that proper nurturing takes place to insure a bountiful crop. If you want to create a new way of life in your organization, you must be patient, consistent, and relentless. It takes years to change an organization's quality mentality. Besides getting everyone trained properly, you need to operate under the new discipline for a few cycles to gain confidence, not only in the system but also in management's commitment to it.

We learn in the parable of the sower that hostile environments can kill even good seeds. The seeds of innovation, service, and quality must be planted in individuals to improve their personal performance. And two things are going to influence that: the soil and the sower. At Toro we've spent a decade cultivating our soil, nurturing and watering it, and digging down to build up topsoil. We have relatively healthy soil now, and our people are also healthier today than they were ten years ago. They care more for their associates, and they value the talents and contributions of others.

We've gone through some bad weather, some recessionary periods that have had a devastating impact on our bottom line. That injured the turf and, to some extent, the soil; new seeds and nutrients were required to restore health. Today, our leaders are prepared not just to broadcast seeds, but to plant those seeds properly, deep down, in rich, well-prepared soil that's been cared for. When they plant the seeds in good, rich soil, the grass will grow abundantly, and processes for continuous improvement will be securely rooted.

Our hope is that the roots will grow deep and strong enough to weather the storms, the hot sun, and whatever other environmental and field conditions we may face. Only then will the combination of the seeds and soil be right, and only then will the harvest prove to be more than the sum of its parts.

Power to Help or Hurt

After collaborating with Janet Hagberg before she published her book, *Real Power,* I concluded that as you become more comfortable with moving power throughout the organization you gravitate to higher levels of power as she defines them. Your power transcends from an outer, symbolic power to an inner power. People with imputed power in an organization often have difficulty pushing it down the hierarchy. Many managers and supervisors covet power and end up emasculating their workforce. It usually takes experience and maturity to realize that an organization is stronger and more productive as power is moved down. As the leader makes this happen, he or she accumulates a deeper power, one from within.

I've been intent for a long time on pushing power down through the layers at Toro. Power exists at all levels of the organization, and there are many ways power can be hoarded or used inappropriately. Hoarding power, for example, helped lead Toro to near-financial crisis in 1981. Our success in the late seventies came about largely from factors outside our control: a strong economy, inflation, and terrific weather, such as blizzards and rainfalls at just the right time. This led to a false sense of our ability to control the market and our position. We were lulled into thinking we were "all powerful." The leadership at Toro attempted to expand, control, and manage without recognizing the other powers that dictated our destinies— such as the innate power of our people, who quietly rebelled against management pressures. Because we appeared to have the power to do it, we expanded imprudently.

Power can be a destructive force if misused or abused. In light of Lord Acton's words, I suppose we should be grateful that none of us has absolute power. I thought about this seriously during a visit with an editor at *Business Week*. He was exploring the question of what happens to people when they become CEOs. His article would examine what power and position do to the CEO. The underlying assumption, I remember thinking, was that a person must inevitably be corrupted in a position of power.

While there have been many glaring and tragic business examples of the abuse of power, I can't agree that it is a *fait accompli*. In fact, I agree with Baltasar Gracian: "The sole advantage of power is that you can do more good." This, it seems to me, is the natural inclination of faithful sowers, dutiful stewards, and servant leaders. When a servant leader becomes the head of an organization, he or she can channel the power in that position to unleash the potential of the people who do the work.

At Toro, our leadership training is focused on using power this way, and managers and leaders are selected and promoted with this in mind. But in the final analysis, a leader must be convinced of the value of the people and the potential of his/her role in unleashing their power. Moreover, the leader must have a bone-deep desire to focus his/her energies toward that goal.

A Leader's Work

There are those who believe that competitiveness in our society, with its ruthless drive to get ahead, is a result of a lack of mutually satisfying relationships. In other words, people who don't have deep relationships may substitute competitiveness and its rewards for personal satisfaction. At the same time, one might argue that competition is often the root cause of our lack of satisfying relationships. When people constantly compete with us, it's hard for us to think of them in positive terms. Likewise, we doubt that they think of us as teammates or associates with whom to align themselves.

Some psychologists contend that these cause-and-effect relationships are circular and self-perpetuating. While self-actualizing people have deeper and more profound interpersonal relationships, people who perceive individual value in terms of "measurable success" tend to lack such satisfying relationships. They're less inclined to interdependency, trust, and humility—traits that seem to characterize self-actualizing individuals. As David Sarnoff, former CEO of RCA, said: "Competition brings out the best in product, but the worst in people." Indeed, when power-hungry, competitive people attain leadership positions, they can do a great deal of harm.

As we define it at Toro, leadership includes such intangibles as inspiration, motivation, courage, patience, strength, perception, gentleness, and compassion. Contrast this with the emotionally sterile and mechanical work environment that many people face today and assume is *natural*—that is, *as it should be.* The current epidemic of "burnout" signals that mammoth change is needed in how leaders get work done. The few executives who lead balanced lives are hailed as gurus possessing extraordinary wisdom, integrity, and ability. And yet they are merely doing what every leader *should* be doing—deploying the right resources to help identify what's wrong and allowing people to participate meaningfully in the solutions.

A leader's work is twofold: to articulate and enroll his constituency in the vision and mission, and to enable the enterprise to move toward targeted destinations using processes that steward its assets, particularly its people assets. Visioning is often intuitive in a leader. Enabling is rarely so simple. Having good systems in place—like having an irrigation system in the ground—makes the job easier. The leader then knows that water can get to the end of every row, that all parts of the organization can receive the necessary ingredients to do their job.

But the systems must be driven by all the people—leaders, managers, supervisors, and employees. Everyone must participate in some sort of synergy to move toward the goal. Because this orchestration is complex and subject to the many vagaries of human nature, the leader must personally demonstrate commitment, discipline, consistency, and trust.

Deep Watering

It's tough for grass to stay green and cool during the heat of the day without deep watering: both in the early morning when the temperature is lower and there is less evaporation, plus periodically during intense heat to reduce heat stress. Deep watering allows a strong root structure to grow.

People, like turf, also need deep watering and strong root structures. Regular deep-watering practices, such as keeping the organization as informed as possible and finding opportunities to reinforce the value system, help employees to weather periods of great stress and uncertainty, like recessions or pressures from change.

Deep watering is similar to the process of building and maintaining the foundation of a work culture; through deep watering employees come to expect and rely on certain behavior patterns and reward systems. Deep watering allows people to operate on a day-to-day basis with a sense of security and trust. They are free to perform on the basis of their abilities, uninhibited by influences from the outside that may dampen their creativity and energy.

As our business began to plummet from the early effects of the 1991 recession, I initiated monthly "recession update" meetings with all employees to inform them of what was happening, what management was thinking, and what to expect. While most of the news reflected the general state of the economy, the meetings reduced uncertainty and added to the sense that we were all one team, all in it together.

In these gatherings, we discussed openly what was happening to our businesses, the impact on our financial picture, and the various responses under consideration. Some might say we took a big gamble in sharing such information with our employees, especially regarding possible layoffs, furlough days, salary cuts, and reorganizations to reduce costs. Like many others, we misjudged the extent of the recession, so for a period the news got worse and worse—and we lost some credibility with our employees. But overall they appreciated knowing our thinking and intentions. They liked hearing that we were trying to preserve the fundamental strengths of the company, including its workforce, in order to restore our momentum as the recession ran its course. I have no doubt that this open communication helped motivate the employees to rally as a corporate team to turn the company around in one year.

A deep-watering program promotes genuine, ongoing involvement enabling people to contribute and be effective, even in the heat of the day. Watering and nurturing foster the conditions that people need in order to grow. To achieve watering and nurturing in a work situation, people development must become as important as corporate productivity. Start with yourself; if you find some means of personal deep watering, you'll improve faster. Every step you take toward self-improvement enables you to be a better leader. You'll become a leader who conscientiously seeks opportunities for learning and who provides opportunities for others to experience deep watering of themselves.

Think of our aerator products as a metaphor. They're used to break up compacted soil below the surface of golf course greens. The purpose of the aerator is to keep the soil fresh and loose so the roots can be revitalized and reach their best depths, making the grass healthier above ground. Other types of aerators are used for decontaminating water, for cleaning silt and solids out of systems, and for getting contaminants out of a system while, at the same time, nourishing roots.

I think of introspection, meditation, and exercise as types of aeration. They're ways of stirring things up below the surface. Once, at the Menninger Clinic in Topeka, I was involved in a six-month self-actualization program that used biofeedback techniques to help participants make better use of their creative and problem-solving capabilities. The concept was that your mental inclinations can, to some degree, cause physical changes within your body. We learned that by focusing our minds on a specific and desired result, we could often mobilize our bodies in that direction. This "stirring" in our minds is the basis for the "mind over matter" idea.

A favorite line of mine is found in Proverbs: "As a man thinketh in his heart, so he is." I also believe that people can do about anything they choose to do. It's not a free ride, nor a slam dunk; it takes work and discipline. But if I expect to help others by being a successful catalyst for growth and success here at Toro, I need to exude that "can do" attitude with enthusiasm. When you engage in deep watering regularly, when you're committed to self-improvement, you tend to stay focused on your goals and pursuits. You discover those elements of your life experience and personal values that can move you forward: to greater insight, to improved leadership, and to opportunities to help others discover their own abilities and potential.

Syringing the Turf

Toro irrigation systems often include a feature that permits the system to "syringe" the grass periodically during the day. In many climates, the early afternoon heat can be intense and can damage the grass, which can be devastating on a golf course. Palm Springs, California, for example, is often called "the golf course capital of the world." In that desert community, there are over eighty golf courses built on sand. In the summer, the temperature commonly exceeds 110 degrees; the grass becomes heat stressed, resulting in burnouts and brown spots. Our irrigation systems, which have been designed to anticipate and avoid these conditions, are installed on many of these courses. When the temperature is high, there's a watering cycle, repeated frequently, that douses the grass and has a cooling effect. Each syringe lasts less than a minute—not enough to interrupt play but enough to keep the grass from burning out.

Similarly, the pace and complexity of work in today's business environment can create sporadic and frequent stress—not necessarily catastrophic, but debilitating and dysfunctional nonetheless. As we constantly change and grow, as we try to do more with less, the organization becomes more stressed. Each new initiative may stretch the organization a little further to achieve some short-term goal, for which most employees may have little appreciation. It is difficult to determine if and when the level of stress enters the red zone. Over time, of course, the stress level becomes an obstacle to productivity. But recognizing a rising stress level is one thing; dealing with it proactively is quite another. Contrary to the first instinct, the solution is not to do less or retrench. That's not reality—nor is it acceptable if you want to keep the enterprise healthy, growing, and competitive. Management needs to apply the principle of "syringing the grasses" to people and their work environment by watering when and where it's needed, and by allowing for a little cooling down during and after the heat of the day, in addition to the soaking that goes on in the evening.

Frequent syringing in times of stress is part of good turf management. It includes things such as helping employees root out low-priority work, recognition, responding quickly to decision requests, eliminating bureaucracy, rolling up your sleeves and working side by side with the production employees on the line or on the customer service desk, being the trainee as well as the trainer, celebrating the myriad of small successes informally, and looking for solutions whereby everyone wins. It's the thousand little things that can positively impact your people.

At Toro, for example, we currently hold informal monthly update meetings with employees called "Huddles with the CEO." I report the progress toward our goals and what we anticipate; I share the successes of the month, recognizing as many people and teams as I can; and I reinforce our strategies, mission, and values. These employee huddles are intended to work like a syringe, to give people hope, a little vision, and some refreshment. As a glimpse of hope, or a picture of the future, the vision and values are only promises and expectations—the superficial syringing during the work period's hectic pace. The deep watering that must necessarily follow must come from all management.

As CEO of a publicly held company, I have to be careful what and how broadly I communicate. But there are many gray areas. In those areas, I exercise my belief that knowledge is power—that an informed workforce works best and most productively for the shareholders. I know our general legal counsel and CFO are often nervous about what I might say during my monthly huddles, but so far I think they would concede the information has been helpful and not inappropriate. Such communication and broad, genuine recognition go a long way in diffusing nonproductive stress. In addition, frequent group lunches hosted by individual executives allow employees to share their concerns as well as their ideas to improve the work climate.

One sweltering summer day when production requirements were high in our Shakopee, Minnesota, plant, the employees had to work in one-hundred-plus-degree temperatures. A group of us filled canisters borrowed from the office cafeteria with lemonade, drove sixteen miles to Shakopee, and served lemonade to all the employees.

Little, seemingly unimportant things such as cold lemonade lift everyone's spirits, especially when unexpected and even when not needed. They help get people through the long, hot spells. It's important to intersperse the regular deep watering with these little cooling off periods. Without them, you can experience bits and pieces of "cultural erosion."

Syringing the grass periodically to alleviate stress vitalizes the organization and reinforces the mission, values, and principles of a company. It is taking a proactive position to preserve and enhance your climate and to direct your leadership toward those people and performance values that support your vision. A good example occurred at Toro in 1990.

During a difficult second quarter, I received inquiries from a company that wanted to buy Toro. We had just purchased Lawn-Boy and the acquisition had depressed our stock. For the first time in ten years, our earnings were projected to be lower than they had been the year before. As far as the public (and many stockholders) could see, it was because of the Lawn-Boy purchase, but there were problems in Toro too.

Because there had been little snowfall that winter, our first quarter wasn't good; I was concerned about our stock value. In December I realized that we were going to have trouble making the financials for the year, and I worried that this would bring negative pressure on our stock, making a takeover attempt all the more appealing. When publicly held companies come out with lower than expected earnings, the stock often tumbles. I visualized a company on the takeover prowl saying, "Here's an opportune time to take a shot at buying Toro, whether they want us to or not."

The situation called for some drastic measures. Without telling anyone why, I simply said, "We've got to make an exception to our product-flow principles and long-term strategies. We need to get shipments out, and we need to cut some expenses now." Some people thought I was going back on my word and making some bad decisions, but because I had built up some trust, most buckled down and put out some extra effort. As a result, the financials we reported for the quarter were acceptable and helped maintain stability in our stock price.

When we reported our quarterly earnings, I decided it was time to gather all employees together in the cafeteria for a little "syringing." Our people had worked long and hard, and it was time to give them a cooling down period, a little celebration, and some recognition to let them know we appreciated their efforts. They had given from deep down, trusting management to do the right thing. They had done a great job. Their team effort had paid off, and we wanted them to know why it was so important. By giving them information and an understanding of why their work had been valuable, and by taking time to share a few moments of celebration together, the "heat stresses" were relieved.

A Way of Life

In turf management, the water has to trickle down through the various layers in the soil to reach the roots. If a layer is compacted, it forms a barrier to the deeper penetration of the water. The roots shrivel and ultimately the grass will die. In watering an organization, unity of purpose is essential because a nonsupportive middle management can create tremendous barriers, and the water will never reach the roots.

At Toro, our biggest challenge has been getting middle management to "live" the culture. If middle management isn't fully enrolled in the culture and enthusiastically supportive—aiding and not impeding the flow of the water through their teams and organizations—I'll hear people saying, "Sure, we heard management talking about it months ago, but nothing has happened since. More words and no action." And they'll be right.

In their defense, middle managers are in a risky position and have the most to lose. If they are still building their careers, struggling to advance, and feeling seemingly contradictory cultural and performance pressures from above, the conflict can be hard to resolve. Middle managers are often drawn back to traditional practices that seemed to work for them in the past. Our middle managers are no different. Senior managers can't dictate cultural behavior, and yet everyone feels the pressure to achieve results.

When we made a conscious decision to adopt our Pride In Excellence corporate culture in 1983, we developed a master culture plan. We identified barriers to building the culture and resistance to meeting objectives at every level. We knew that this change had to be more than a program that runs its course and ends in a year or two. If it was viewed as a program, employees would expect it to fade and perhaps be replaced with another, more contemporary program. It had to be positioned and seen as a way of life. And it had to be owned by all, not seen as Ken Melrose's culture.

We wanted to enroll everyone in the philosophy, and we started with the first-line managers, the officers. We knew some of the officers needed to change their management styles and beliefs about people. Their management styles were autocratic and often devaluing, sometimes without their knowing it. They were good results-oriented managers who had performed well against quantitative objectives. The "what" they accomplished had been impressive; it was the "how" that concerned us.

We enrolled three officers in a management-style awareness and development program to modify the way they interfaced and interacted with people. The "how" of leadership became as important as the "what" of their responsibilities. Knowing they were solid people with some behavioral practices that were out of sync with our cultural values, we felt we should give them a chance to clearly see the impact of their style and practices on others and understand the consequences of that style in the new Toro culture. We wanted them to explicitly understand what we were looking for, and then give them a year to see if we (as well as their subordinates) could observe measurable, positive change.

We set some objectives with them and explained thoroughly that if the objectives were not met we were prepared to help them find an environment more compatible with their style. We needed them to represent the company in a way that would fully support the Pride In Excellence culture. If they were to be part of Toro's future, they needed to visibly adopt and embrace the new culture. They needed to demonstrate the values articulated in the corporate vision. Two of those three managers are still at Toro. The third, before finally departing, assumed a consulting responsibility that utilized his technical skills but took him out of the interpersonal mainstream. In all three cases, I believe we were clear, fair, and valuing to the managers as human beings.

It has not been all roses. A female administrator was terminated in one of our plants. She was a very good person; I remember her using CPR to save someone's life at a company picnic. Despite her good work, there were performance problems. Her supervisors had spoken with her several times; they had tried to work out the difficulties that eventually led to her termination.

She wrote me a letter questioning her termination. In particular, she felt the way her situation had been handled was inconsistent with our professed cultural values. After I looked into both sides of the story, I concluded that her termination was justified. I wrote her back to say that we did indeed demonstrate Pride In Excellence by our action. I wrote, "There were some specific performance problems even you admitted to, and at the least, were clearly spelled out on more than one occasion. Pride In Excellence should value every individual, but it also means honoring the whole organization. If we allow continually poor performance by one person after providing direction and support to change, it's hard for us to request and expect excellent performance from others. If we had let you stay on and allowed you to continue to perform the way you were, we would not have valued the rest of the organization, and would have been doing them and you a disservice in the long run." I never heard from her again.

Pride In Excellence has become partly a symbol and partly a mandate to treat each other respectfully and to recognize everyone's value and worth to the organization. Yes, there are times when you have to hold people's feet to the fire and manage more directly with less consensus, especially times of crisis. Management is an integration of valuing people and valuing performance to achieve the vision.

I firmly believe you can achieve results while still honoring a process that values the employee's worth. There are going to be times you have to terminate someone. Management's responsibility is to minimize these occasions by insuring clear expectations, good coaching, and a reward process that focuses on recognizing contributions. When the manager doesn't do that, the problem often shows up at the grassroots level.

We anticipated that some managers would have problems and that every Toro employee would need time to adapt. We realized, too, that people—in whatever position they held—could not and would not adapt without making a personal commitment to the PIE culture. Rather than force an artificial compliance that would satisfy no one, a parting of the ways was sometimes better for everyone involved.

For leaders, the philosophy of a people-valuing culture must become an integral part of their walk and talk. Leaders can't assume that culture is something for the general employee population but not for themselves. In fact, culture is something for management to advance, and it won't work if management only gives lip service in the hope of facilitating more or better work out of the people on the line.

We try to focus managers' goal-setting activities on performance requirements. We ask each officer, director, and leader to develop his or her own "culture plan" around our six people-values. We also ask our associates, subordinates, and supervisors to set goals for their leaders—and then to evaluate the leader's accomplishments against these goals at the end of the year. These evaluations quickly expose those managers who only pay lip service to our corporate values, and they identify the departments that are deprived of the right leadership models. The values of Pride In Excellence need constant, consistent, comprehensive communication and matching behavior on the part of all involved. The culture has to be a way of life, and you can't get there without putting real energy behind it.

In the traditional working culture, people "just do a job." Management controls, directs, and possibly rides roughshod over employees, who are viewed as unimportant people who carry out necessary but equally unimportant duties. In such a culture, even if we don't realize it, the law of the harvest still determines the outcomes. Over time, you get little return when you don't invest much. In Second Corinthians, we read: "If you give little, you will get little. A farmer who plants just a few seeds will get only a small crop, but if he plants much, he will reap much." Inevitably, lack of investment in people results in depreciation in value of this most important asset, which will lead to business deterioration. As people become more and more disgruntled, cynical, or apathetic, you'll get higher turnover and a large replacement cost, not to mention the huge opportunity loss from the diminished contribution of those who stay.

Our turnover has consistently been half the national average, and I'm grateful that most of our people find the grass is greener on our side of the fence. They make it green by embracing loyalty, teamwork, and service commitment. Their experience provides more innovation. And more often, they rise to their potential so they'll be better tomorrow than they were yesterday. As with any asset of value, you have to continually invest in your people in order to improve their worth.

Conditions for Culture Growth

I believe that people want to perform, and are capable of performing, if the boss and the system will let them do their best work. The goal of *productivity through people* is achieved by treating people as partners worthy of respect and dignity. In *Control Your Own Destiny, or Someone Else Will,* Noel Tichy says, "I'm convinced that the most effective competitors will be the organizations that learn how to use shared values to harness the emotional energy of employees. As speed, quality, and productivity become ever more important, corporations need people who can instinctively act the right way, without instructions, and who feel inspired to share their best ideas with their employers."

Don Beveridge, a popular motivational consultant who worked with us at Toro during our rebuilding period, also believes that the competitive edge in a company is the excellence, empathy, and expertise of the people you employ. He challenged us with the phrase, "If it's to be, it's up to me!" and helped us translate that charge into empowerment actions.

What can executives do to create the right conditions for a winning culture and for individual peak performance? What can a coach do to put a winning team on the turf? What can leaders do to make the people who work in the trenches and in the field feel part of the network? How can a CEO help create conditions that are right for growth, performance, creativity, and quality?

I don't have all the answers, but this much I do know: Leadership must be genuine. Artificial or contrived styles simply don't work because people know when they're being patronized. They know when they're being manipulated. You have to build an organization on a foundation of trust, one step at a time. If you have built a trusting organization, you have great power. You and your organization are both able to accomplish goals and do exceptional things. You can begin executing the disciplines of excellence in performance, whether it's total quality or world-class manufacturing or superior customer service.

In a culture that values the "seed not sod" principle, power and decision-making authority are diffused throughout the organization, and clear objectives and expectations are communicated to everyone—customers and suppliers as well as employees. All stakeholders are held accountable for their specific contribution and role. In shaping supportive and productive cultures, leaders may launch certification programs for suppliers, enroll customers in company quality initiatives, and value employees in various ways. Most importantly, leaders must seek regular feedback and conduct frequent audits to deal effectively with the inevitable problems, misunderstandings, and subpar performances.

We have several feedback mechanisms in place at Toro. In my "PIE à la Toro" meetings with employees, I ask them to fill out a short questionnaire to check the pulse of the culture. Their concerns then become top-of-mind issues that we discuss during the meeting. I also review all of our exit interviews. Because people leaving have no reason to couch their phrases or pick their terms, exit interviews provide a great way to identify true attitudes within the company. In addition, members of our Pride In Excellence action team act as catalysts for the culture, informally reporting on the temperature of the company. More recently, officers are conducting their own culture audits to identify concerns and ideas within their groups. All of this feedback is periodically consolidated to give us an overview of the employee temperature. It's part of a continuous improvement process.

It's important to recognize and value people at the grassroots level, where much of the real work is done. In fact, the idea of "giving up" power to people at lower levels is, in a way, a fallacy because that's where the real power has been all the time. Power is with people who design and build products, deliver results, process information, and deal directly with customers and suppliers. They have the facts, they're in the line of fire, and they know what works and what doesn't.

Don Shula, coach of the Miami Dolphins and professional football's most winning coach by the end of the 1993 season, has always been a practitioner of "bottom-up power." Though Shula is regarded as a perfectionist, he knew where to turn to help achieve his team's goals. As Jim Langer, a Dolphins "Wall-of-Fame" offensive lineman of the seventies, reported to Minneapolis sportswriter Curt Brown: "It wasn't uncommon for Don to call a bunch of us linemen together and say 'Okay, guys, which plays do you think will work best against the Steelers?' So we'd go to work, do our own film study, and decide which plays we thought best suited us. Don allowed that kind of exchange because he recognized he wasn't an expert on how to block Joe Greene. He allowed input from those of us who did know."

Like Shula, I start with my staff. Then they have to work with their teams. And then their teams work with the plant management, or the engineers, or the salespeople. Plant managers have to work with the plant supervisors, and so on. We work with those who were once viewed as adversaries but are now seen as allies. And the best way to make allies out of adversaries is to practice the principles of servant leadership.

CHAPTER EIGHT

The Leader
as Servant

Leadership is action, not position.
— DONALD MCGANNON

FOR MANY YEARS, I've collected various sayings or adages that strike a chord with me. These quotes paint a fairly good picture of who and what I've tried to be and how I've tried to live my life. The Master of Men fittingly expressed the ideal of leadership in a democracy when he said, "Whoever wants to be great among you must be your servant." In my opinion, these few words from the New Testament can stand up against all the management books on the shelves today. The great leader is a great servant.

Although the model of the leader as servant has been in the canons of management for years, in actual practice it's still rare. I believe that without strong models of servant leaders, a person is hard pressed to put the principles of servant leadership into practice. Fortunately, I had great models.

While I was growing up, my parents struggled financially. My dad ran a laundromat. Later, he became a real estate broker and then a stockbroker. My mother helped support the family by teaching at a junior high school. My parents couldn't afford to send my older brother to Princeton, but he received a scholarship and worked serving meals to other students. By the time I was ready for college, my mother had inherited a little money, which she had wisely invested in stocks. The money from those investments paid for my education at Princeton.

My parents set very high standards of excellence. These were things we discussed at the dinner table, and I was expected to perform to those high standards. If I didn't meet them, we didn't celebrate "good tries" with crepe paper streamers or balloons. I became a perfectionist in many ways because I couldn't stand not pleasing my parents, and I came to believe that my worth was somehow tied up with my performance and achievements. As a high achiever, I was pretty hard on myself when I fell short of my own expectations.

I began my professional life with a low tolerance for incompetency, stemming I'm sure from my upbringing. Because I was aware of this disposition, I worked hard to become more empathetic in interpersonal relationships. I tried to understand the other person's point of view first, especially when I had a different opinion. My natural inclination was to blurt out my ideas, but I've learned to try someone else's ideas on for size first.

Early in my career, when I was working for The Pillsbury Company as a marketing manager, the director of marketing used to tell me, "Realize that you are the 'flexible' resource and the other person is the 'fixed' resource." As a result I worked to be flexible and tried to relate to how other people were feeling. That's a lot easier when you care about the other person. When you value other people, the desire and willingness to understand and empathize are much greater. I care deeply about the people of Toro. I try to get to know them personally and let them know they are appreciated.

While I try to be empathetic, demonstrating humanness, warmth, and good listening skills has not always been easy for me.

Frankly, I have had to work at it. Now I take more time with people who want to talk. I listen to them. What they have to say doesn't have to be earth-shattering. What's important is to take a few minutes out of the day to share one-on-one with another human being. I try to focus on their eyes and face. I listen to their words and try to understand their emotions. These exchanges keep me informed, but what's more significant is the reminder of what is really important in life: to be in meaningful, caring relationships. Many things in life are taken care of if we nurture and enrich our relationships, both personal and professional.

PIE à la Toro

As CEO, I'm the servant. Since 1985 I've held a monthly meeting with fifteen or so employees. We call it "PIE à la Toro." We get together in a conference room or in my office and have lunch; sometimes we even have pie. But the reason for the meetings is to talk informally, to allow employees to discuss what is on their minds. It gives me a chance to ask how they feel about Toro, their jobs, and our direction. I encourage other officers to do this, too, promising them that, "You'll get a feeling for what's happening, a pulse that's unfiltered and natural, if you open up and talk about whatever anyone wants to talk about."

These get-togethers give us a chance to relate to each other in a different way. They help us to break down barriers. I can be Ken Melrose, the person—somebody sitting around the table having lunch with everyone else. The conversation is warm and natural. We don't just talk Toro. Sometimes we talk about other things, whatever comes into our minds.

I also have informal meetings or lunch in my office with new employees as part of their orientation. Periodically, I invite new employees to my office. We introduce ourselves, and then I tell them a little bit about Toro. I make a point of asking them to tell me what their first weeks at Toro have been like. I ask everyone to share with me what they think about Toro, and to compare their experience at Toro with their past experiences.

Invariably, they comment on the sense of family they feel here. Many describe our culture as "a caring environment." I invite them to talk about their work group and associates. "They're so cooperative, receptive, and helpful" are common remarks. They talk about the freedom they feel. They talk about the importance of name tags, and how helpful they are in getting to know everyone around you quickly because they let you put a name and a face together. For most of them, it's the first time they've ever owned stock, so they'll talk about the sense of ownership they feel. Very often I hear that they never met their former company's CEO, not even in several years of working there, not to mention having lunch in the CEO's office.

That's when I'm most aware that our new employees experience a sort of culture shock when they come to Toro. They report definite, discernible differences—some of which people who have been here for years may no longer perceive. New employees talk about their sense of belonging. They talk about the company's mission and how they perceive their role in it. They talk about their feelings for employee involvement, commitment, and participation. It reminds me of the keen observations grandparents make when visiting their grandchildren; they notice every change. Because of daily contact, it's difficult for a mom and dad to discern the small changes in a child's growth and behavior, but grandparents who visit infrequently see the children with new eyes and see big changes.

Sometimes, after our meeting, I might hear people say, "I was nervous about meeting with the CEO today." This statement reminds me of the barrier my position creates. There is, of course, a necessary level of assigned leadership. At the same time, the position inhibits in others the freedom to risk, brainstorm ideas, and be who they really are. It creates the false sense that I'm better and more worthy than others, which is unfortunate. Yet I think of my roots and who I am, and I think, "But I'm just like you are. What's the difference?"

Sometimes I'll conduct an exit interview. Only rarely do I find a reason for leaving like, "I got a raw deal from my boss," or "I've been devalued." Usually people leave because of a family transfer or a quicker or larger promotional opportunity. It's not because of the benefits or the environment. People tell me, "I hate to leave." They, and we, feel a real separation. Sometimes when you talk to these same people years later, they'll say, "Well, I gave up a lot for a little more money." Or, "I wish I could come back. The environment in my new job isn't what it was at Toro."

Over the last four decades, the concept of the hierarchical boss has turned around 180 degrees—from controlling, to telling, to directing, to guiding, to coaching, and finally to serving. In his earlier presentations, Tom Peters would depict the structural change through an inverted organizational chart with the customer at the top as boss, the employees working for the customers, and management working under the employees to serve or satisfy the needs of the customers. The servant-leader model requires a change in attitude more than a structural change, however. To genuinely operate in this mode, leaders have to shed their egos and deep in their bones embrace the belief that they best serve the goals of the enterprise by allowing employees to do what they do best in an atmosphere of freedom, trust, and recognition. More importantly, to sustain this practice, leaders must genuinely believe in the value and potential of each employee.

Becoming a Servant Leader

In *Stronger Than Steel,* Wayne Alderson, former operating head of Pittron Steel, describes how he learned that serving his people unleashed their creativity, motivation, and capabilities, and directed them toward the goals of the company. A World War II veteran who survived a foxhole grenade explosion, Alderson later played a key role in the survival of a small Pennsylvania steel company, Pittron Steel. The company was threatened in part by a protracted conflict between management and union employees. Alderson maintains that the company was actually saved by itself; his servant leadership merely allowed it to happen. He provided sound guidelines and direction, trusted his employees to contribute as he knew they could, and then held them all accountable.

Pittron Steel was able to save itself once the workers realized their leader genuinely valued them, not only as employees with a job to do but also as human beings. When they began to trust, their potential contributions were unleashed, saving Pittron from the brink of financial failure and eventually making the company a competitive U.S. steel manufacturer. Alderson was a leader who served his employees not because he knew he would get more out of them, but because he wanted them to recognize their self-worth and dignity, and wanted to help them become better human beings. That's what servant leadership is all about.

Leadership is not a position; it's a combination of something you are (character) and some things you do (competence). Suppose a man who works in a Toro production plant focuses his energies on what he does and over time gets very good at it. Suppose that he and I went through high school together, but now years later, he works on the line and I'm CEO. People may think, "Well, if Ken Melrose gets paid fourteen times more than Joe, Melrose must be fourteen times better. He's the boss." If I buy into this kind of thinking, I'm perpetuating the myth of leadership as a position.

Leadership can be coveted by people for the wrong reasons; some seem to thrive on enhanced personal identity and power, others may have a need to assert their presumed greater value, and make it clear to everyone who's in control. Words such as chief, director, and executive officer have a nice ring to them, and the attendant benefits aren't bad either. But if we think of leadership as a position, it's almost impossible to develop an environment of trust. People who worry about preserving personal power aren't likely to accept the idea of "leader as servant." They aren't likely to give up power to benefit everyone involved, or even to understand the concept. Any service they give in the name of that concept is going to be lip service, and the moment they feel threatened, they're going to yank "their power" back and hold onto it hard.

Leadership is as much an art as it is a science. As such, it's far from black and white. Very often, the issues we face are subtle and unclear. Then, too, there are times when the issue is clear enough, but we have blinders on. The Watergate experience shows plainly that ordinary men, just "doing their jobs," may accept assignments handed down from their supervisors without questioning the right or wrong involved. Or, even if they do question the moral correctness of their orders, what kind of world is it where a leader's values can be compromised by ambition or concerns over job security?

We have, hopefully, moved out of the period when blind obedience was expected, and into a time when the concept of empowerment—moving responsibility, accountability, ownership, and power down in an organization—is receiving support in the workplace. The individual is empowered to try, to fail or succeed, and to take another step toward the goal. In this way, even failure can be goal-directed. Each of us does the best we can within a host of constraints.

Whenever we step in front of the crowd and say, "Follow me," the implication is that we know where we're going and what we want to achieve. The assumption is that we're committed to give our very best efforts. Knowing that personal values influence the quality of leadership, we must ask ourselves: Will my values enable me and my followers to arrive at our goals with our integrity and self-esteem intact and stronger than ever? If a leader can't offer integrity and consistent values, especially in times of crisis, followers will dwindle. As the saying goes: "Every now and then, a leader ought to look back to see if anyone is following."

My question is this: If you fail to measure yourself and benchmark your performance against your best visions, norms, and standards, how can you do more than pretend to lead, and how can you expect to impart vision and higher expectations to others? Leaders set the tone for everything that occurs within their organizations. For this reason, leaders must give careful attention to the stories they're writing with their deeds. As you help to write your company's story, remember you have it within your power to help your company develop a new culture—with a climate of trust that is defined by a set of values that stresses the dignity and importance of every employee. This is the service you can best offer your company as a leader.

You don't have to be the perfect example of all the disciplines of excellence, especially if the corporation is firmly behind you and has sufficient forward momentum to carry you past your own weaknesses. In fact, your imperfections may enhance your humanness and thereby help set the tone for risks, innovation, and trust. What you do need is a firm commitment to a personal development program and dedication to continuous improvement. I'm well aware that I'm in no way a perfect model, but I'm committed to continuous learning and growing. I'm also confident that Toro will stand as a fine example of a learning organization with a climate of trust.

Manage Your Turf Well

Over the years at Toro, I've learned a few things about managing the turf, both inside the company and out on the grass. If you think of your turf as your domain—as the environment you operate in—then your turf becomes your area of influence. Turf may also refer to your organization, your work area, your home and garden, or whatever domain you occupy.

Toro's mission and purpose have been broadened from a "lawn and garden" equipment manufacturer to an "environmental improvement" equipment manufacturer. During the eighties, we established a subsidiary, Toro Ventures International (TVI), that helped redefine and broaden some of our businesses. A utility vehicle business, water aeration, and a line of probiotic fertilizers, all now growing nicely as part of Toro, were outgrowths of TVI's initiatives. In addition, the Irrigation Division began moving toward water management, with a particular focus on remediation, and our recently acquired Kansas subsidiary, which manufactures tub grinders (large circular tubs with heavy rotating steel knives that grind up organic refuse), is becoming an outdoor recycling equipment business.

Toro Ventures has also been responsible for putting Toro in the water aeration business through some joint ventures. The water aerator's purpose is to oxygenate a stagnant or contaminated lake or pond, allowing good bacteria to grow and eat up all the pollution.

An in-place aerator produces a relatively clean pond in thirty days. We're installing these systems on golf courses now.

An executive can also be an aerator, cleaning up a polluted or stagnant environment as we did at Toro. Despite our long-standing reputation for quality, our product was not up to Toro standards and many of our assets had not grown in value. The people, the physical facilities, the plants, the equipment, and the product all had defects. The challenge was to air out the company and add fresh life, new hope, and vision.

In *Why Am I Afraid to Love?*, John Powell charges us to ask of others, "What do you need me to be today?" Powell learned painfully that leaders need to be the flexible resource when dealing with others, and develop their empathic skills. "What does the organization, my everyday world, need me to be today: a coach, a teacher, a decision maker, a supporter, a listener, a pilgrim, a servant, someone who makes waves?" Since the needs of the organization and its constituents change daily, leaders need to be continually learning. In a sense, every leader is in the discovery and rediscovery business.

The servant-leader model is not an easy model to embrace. But the style permits the greatest number of people to experience the greatest good. In the servant-leader model, the leader's role is to provide optimal conditions for the growth, development, and self-improvement of all. If you are to do that, you must find and unleash new powers from within yourself, and empower others to do the same. You must discover new perspectives, commitment, and passions within yourself, and inspire your followers to make their own discoveries. As a leader, you must tap into your inner strengths. You must share the power and spirit you discover there with others, for the benefit of all.

CHAPTER NINE

The Importance of Trust

Always operate under the premise that the best solution may be outside the environment being considered, and assume your resources have the ability to stretch beyond current boundaries.

— ANONYMOUS

OUR PRIDE IN EXCELLENCE culture is based on my belief and my trust that people want to do the right thing. After fifteen years I still believe this because I've seen proof of it time and time again. I also believe that every employee—whether in the office, in the warehouse, or on the production line—wants to provide quality products and services in which he or she can take personal pride. I have seen many of our employees move in directions and take on responsibilities that no one, including themselves, could have imagined when they began at Toro. Trust is the element that makes this possible.

Building trust is a long-term proposition; it's a marathon, not a sprint. I've told the folks at Toro on several occasions that our trusting and valuing culture will reach its peak in sixty years. It's a sixty-year "program"! I want people to know that Toro will still be building this culture well beyond their retirement. (I originally wanted to use a time frame of fifty years, but I noticed that we had employees who had celebrated their fiftieth anniversary with Toro and were still working productively!)

Having a long-term orientation is so critical to the growth of our culture that I've made it one of my key roles to provide constant focus, training, support, and communications in order to keep the cultural conduit open. Consequently, most of our managers give people the time to do the right thing and coach them along the way through the right processes. They recognize that the fruits are more significant and rewarding, yet take longer to blossom.

Building trust follows the law of nature. You can't "cram" as you might cram for a test in school. The farmer can't cram; he must align himself with the laws of nature, not simply improve processes and systems or use the latest technology. He must go through the process of preparing the soil, seeding the soil, and nurturing the root structure and subsequent sprouts of grass before the harvest occurs.

Preventive Maintenance

In the early eighties, soon after I became president, I tried to be the prime mover of the culture. I took responsibility for teaching our people to value their customers and asked them to report to me on customer requirements. I saw this as preventive maintenance, reasoning that an employee who cared about the product and his/her work would always do the right thing to achieve quality and excellence. As it turned out, some of the managers between my office and the employees hadn't actually bought into the culture. This meant that people on the line and in the office received different messages from their supervisors (quantity and quotas) than from me (quality and teamwork).

Quality and teamwork usually lost out because the supervisor had more information and more direct power than I did. I decided I needed to make sure *all* the management level people at Toro understood and acted on my preventive maintenance concept. Otherwise, whose words could employees trust and how could they function at their true capability levels? I wanted management to be responsible to train and support their people in preventive maintenance causing the philosophy to cascade down through the layers of hierarchy and culture.

It took us a long time to achieve that. Every company has those who can't accept or behave in accordance with the value system. These individuals are better off in a more compatible work environment, and so is your company. But it's hard to identify all the naysayers; they don't just come out and say, "Nuts to that," at least not within earshot. You have to watch carefully for negative behaviors and constantly repeat your expectations. We had to coach and counsel some people who couldn't buy in. From top to bottom, we ended up replacing people who weren't committed to the culture. While it always hurts to lose people, the culture and Toro were stronger for having taken the loss.

Even now when I start talking about goals and vision, culture and values, ideas and initiatives, some employees are cynical. They'll say, "We've heard this before," or "Well, we'll wait and see." Then they sit on the sidelines and don't participate. Some even fuel the negative flames with apathy or subtle sabotage. Eventually, these people leave the company, but before they do, they inhibit the development of the organization and consequently the company's pursuit of its goals. It's important to identify them and get them either on or off the ship.

Building Trust at Toro

I believe Shakespeare's words: "Sweet are the uses of adversity." When the recession hit, when the weather turned against us, when the competition got intense, and when customer standards rose even higher, it left little room for the waste and inefficiency that come from hierarchical processes like constant approvals, meetings, reviews, updating, and reports. People had to respond to the market, their legs churning as they hit the deck. Management had to trust that people were doing the right things. Trust—at all levels of the organization—became more important then ever.

Under these conditions, we could see that the heroes in the company were not only the high-profile people, nor the top sales leaders, nor the product innovators. There were many behind-the-scenes heroes who worked at preventing problems and preparing breakthroughs long before a product goes to market. In a strong organization, everyone is a hero of some sort. We discovered and rediscovered the value of recognizing all the silent, unspoken heroes who go about their jobs without complaint.

I like the story Roger Milliken tells about one of his plant people who wanted a business card of her own and a title that reflected her own view of her job and value. He said she could be anything she wanted, so she had the company make her a set of cards with her name and the title "Supreme Commander" underneath her name. Here was one of Milliken's many heroes who wanted to be recognized as such, and Roger said, "You bet!"

If you, as a leader, want to build trust in an organization, you have to begin with a genuine belief that your people are valuable and important. At Toro, our leaders believe that our employees are the people that make the company successful, and they behave accordingly. When I retire, I would like to sing "The Wind Beneath My Wings," the song Bette Midler popularized in the movie *Beaches*, to all the Toro employees. I doubt I'll have the courage to do it, but "I was the one with all the glory, while [they] were the ones with all the strength." At Toro, I was able to "fly higher than an eagle, 'cause [they] were the wind beneath my wings."

As a leader, you can't let your people stay "cold there in your shadow." Jack Welch of General Electric claims he repeatedly learned recognition was a key to the success of his collaborative teaming initiative called "Work-Out." We, too, discovered and rediscovered the value of recognizing all the silent, unspoken heroes who go about their jobs without complaint, "only a face, without a name." It's part of the "preventive maintenance" philosophy, and leaders need to make it a part of every plan and every solution. Trust is the element that makes this possible. And recognition breeds more trust.

Sometimes the CEO has to clear the air by saying, "What's done is done; yes, we made mistakes, but today we are facing a new challenge and our job is to meet it. We have no other choice." At Toro, we've had to do this more than once. For example, for a number of years we had engaged in practices that eroded our foundation. As a publicly held company, we reported financial performance each quarter, creating enormous pressure to maximize short-term results. That and the lure of Wall Street led us into a preoccupation with accelerated growth in sales—partly accomplished by stealing from the future.

To recover the ground we had lost, management had to own up to past mistakes and make some hard commitments, and then we had to live with them. That taught us to be very careful indeed about the commitments we make. For example, during the period in the eighties when we operated within our bank consortium's master credit agreement, we calculated carefully what we were absolutely sure we could do, and then committed to nothing else. We didn't talk about other things we'd like to do or hoped to do because we were afraid we would be able to do only 80 percent of them. Our lenders needed to see results coincident with our projections in each and every period. At that time, imposing a very specific and clear vision, persevering tenaciously toward that vision, and keeping everyone moving down that path were necessary for survival. Sticking to and achieving what we said we'd do made the banks come around, to the tune of $140 million of working capital loans. Every quarter, we delivered exactly what we had budgeted—no more, no less. Very importantly, we were beginning to build trustworthiness with some of our primary stakeholders—our lenders and our employees.

As the eighties progressed, we began seeding for the future instead of stealing from the future. Recognizing our business was seasonal and that virtually all our product sales were affected by weather, we began to budget a contingency reserve of roughly 1 percent of sales. That way we could buffer our financial statements against normal upsets and still stay on plan. Then as the end of the quarter or year neared, we'd start seeding the next period by postponing savings and sales to the future, as long as we could achieve our current targets. When we came to the end of the year, we'd ask, "How can we insure that next year will be strong? Why don't we move some expenses up into this year? Why don't we write off more obsolete inventory? Why don't we get our shipments closer to the end-user requirements by moving some sales into the future?" As we tried to rebuild our balance sheet, we were conservative in our planning each year, so we invariably ended up with more than we needed. We were able to move some extra opportunity into the future and gradually all of Toro discovered the value of the principle, seed not sod.

How can you pull off seeding for the future when you're living in an American culture that has the lowest savings rate of any developed nation—in a culture where the buzzwords on every TV commercial are quick, simple, now, free, and instant? In his best-selling book, *The Road Less Traveled,* M. Scott Peck makes a compelling case for delayed gratification, but it's a hard sell when the "seed not sod" idea is counter to virtually everything we experience in our day-to-day lives. How do you get people to understand *we, team, seed,* and *wait* when their cultural environment and media messages are telling them just the opposite?

I believe you do it by letting people decide for themselves how to do something. You don't go to employees and constituents and say, "We need to sacrifice now for the long term, so I want all of you to wait until the ship comes in." A better way is to ask them, "What do you think is the best way to do this?" When they answer, you listen. You try to ratify their conclusions and help put them into action.

At Toro, we're trying to lead differently. We recognize that real power is where the action is: where the orders are taken; where the parts are punched, welded, and painted; where the invoices are cut; and where the facts and data are. We move decision-making power to individual employees and teach them how to use it to achieve better decisions, greater productivity, and real ownership.

I've discovered that the impetus for the most productive activities at Toro typically comes from the lower levels in the organization. For example: A computer user group created high productivity not only by using PCs and LANs (local area networks), but also by sharing productivity enhancement tools and defining their training needs; and an office clerical group figured out how to make better use of administrative staff who have highs and lows in their work time by forming a network pool to work on special projects during slack periods.

The Toro culture tries to drive power down to the people who do the actual work and really make things happen. For this reason, I always operate under the premise that the best solution may be outside the environment being considered—somewhere outside the normal realms of management. But I assume that my resources have the ability to stretch the current boundaries.

In his "Work-Out" teaming initiative, Jack Welch, CEO of General Electric, charges his cross-functional teams to operate in environments without boundaries. That's the right idea. Moving the boundaries outward opens up a host of new options for solutions. So my task, and your task as a leader, is to create an atmosphere that enables this boundary stretching. Why? Because no matter how good the leadership is, or how smart the management is, the results are only as good as the execution. And people can only execute when they have access to the best ideas and alternatives.

Beyond Traditional Boundaries

Our employees and our distributors made it possible for Toro to recover from a potentially suicidal path. We hoped we were looking at a win-win situation; a long-term "win-win" situation, however, can be perceived in the beginning by one partner as a short-term win-lose. This was the case in August 1989 when we wanted to buy Cushman-Ryan, the leader in turf utility vehicles for the golf course market.

Cushman-Ryan was then owned by OMC (Outdoor Marine Corp.). Our objective was to combine the utility vehicles with our turf maintenance equipment, also primarily for the golf course market. Our premise was that since Cushman-Ryan had a monopoly on utility vehicles in the golf segment, our distributors would gain new entries into this very important market, thereby expanding the penetration of our existing equipment lines.

The purchase of Cushman-Ryan would cost $150 million, which would overly leverage our balance sheet and put Toro at some risk. As a result, we decided to do an off-balance-sheet purchase, showing it as a leveraged buyout venture. To do that, we would need to raise $18 million of equity capital through a 50/50 joint venture with another party. The key was to find someone who could both quickly come up with the money and be a real partner with us. We soon realized the obvious and only conceivable "partner" was our distributor organization. After all, since they were essential to our selling strategies, who better to share the risks and rewards? Toro would put up half the $18 million, and the distributors would put up the other half.

So the first day of our annual distributor sales convention, we gathered together all our distributors, and I said, "Look, we'll need commitments from each of you. I need $9 million in total—and I need to know in two days whether or not I can get it." Two days later, we had signed commitments for $11 million. The distributors knew very little about Cushman-Ryan's financial situation or the condition of its business; there was no time for them to do their "due diligence." They signed on faith, in effect saying, "Well, if Toro wants us to do it, we'll do it. If they think this is the right thing to do, we'll support them. If it will be good for them, it'll be good for us." And so on a wing and a prayer, we came away with $11 million. There are not many companies who can do that, and there are even fewer companies that have the close and trusting relationships we have with our distributors: partnerships that have been forged over the last fifty years.

Eventually we lost the bid for Cushman-Ryan to a competitor, but we won something more valuable—the reaffirmation of the bond of trust between Toro and an important partner. This story illustrates the level of trust from years of seeding and careful nurturing on Toro's part. It was the fruition of decades of effort to cultivate, deep water, diligently maintain, and even beautify a relationship so that in a time of crisis, one partner was there to help the other. All the work paid off. The natural seasons and cycles of growth and development do bear fruit. I'm still awed to know that when it's needed we can go to our distributors and raise millions of dollars on our word alone.

This story also illustrates a solution that we found outside of our preconceptions, outside of the normal finance environment. We didn't know at first that our capital resources would stretch beyond the Toro boundaries to include our relationship with our distributors. We do now. But it was no easy task to create an atmosphere that allowed us to stretch that far, and it would have been foolish to expect it to be easy. It was worth every bit of cultivating and watering that it took, and our efforts yielded good fruit for our labors.

We began building trust with our constituents when we began honoring our commitments repeatedly—commitments to our banks, to our employees, and to our customers. Every commitment fulfilled added to the growing level of trust. Stephen Covey uses the idea of "emotional bank accounts" to talk about building trust. We all have accounts with our associates, and as they or we meet promises or expectations, deposits are made to the accounts. Withdrawals occur each time a commitment made is not fulfilled. We realized the fragility of our trust accounts—every missed commitment would deplete a little of the trust in the bank.

During the eighties, we were very cognizant of how our PIE culture could help build trust within the organization too. Because we recognized our employees as responsible adults and valuable associates, we felt they were entitled to information and management's thinking about the company. Open and forthright communication was a very important part of our culture. That's why we initiated the monthly recession updates to inform the employees about Toro's situation when our business was rapidly declining. The more we communicated in this way, the more employees came to believe in what management was saying.

Being fair and compassionate is also key in building trust. Balancing results and relationships, setting examples, leading the sacrifices, celebrating "good tries" when the results are unfavorable, all help create a sense of security, especially important during rapid change or crisis. This, of course, leads to more trust.

The PIE culture asks our management to be more human with the employees—to flex to their level in the organization. That's one reason we initiated the idea of management working in each plant for a day each year or so. On that day it becomes perfectly clear that the officers can't perform the assembly or fabrication jobs as well as the plant people can. And the employees love seeing that we aren't the experts in their domain that they are.

Management often serves pie or coffee at celebrations, passes out dividend checks or turkeys, and performs other symbolic gestures that suggest we work for the employees, not the other way around. These cultural activities honor the value and worth of others and engender trust in both directions.

Trust is the key! It is really the glue that bonds the organization together. It is the foundation upon which all other organizational attributes germinate and grow, such as freedom to fail, risk taking, empowerment, honesty, and openness. When you have trust in your organization, you can achieve anything!

CHAPTER TEN

Breaking
Barriers

The real barrier wasn't in the sky, but in our
knowledge and experience of supersonic flight.
— GENERAL CHUCK YEAGER

IN 1988, RECOVERY MADE IT POSSIBLE for Toro to crack the Fortune
500 barrier for the first time. Because we thought of ourselves as a
small, closely knit company, it was a major achievement for us, something like breaking the sound barrier for the first time. When Chuck
Yeager attempted that feat in 1947, no one knew what to expect
because no one had ever done it. The real barrier, as it turned out,
was mostly mental.

When Yeager wanted to crack the sound barrier and its "invisi-
ble brick wall," some prominent scientists claimed they had hard
data that proved the barrier was impenetrable. Others predicted that
both pilot and plane would disintegrate at Mach 1, or that the pilot
would lose his voice, revert in age, or be severely buffeted.
Notwithstanding, on that historic day, Yeager attained an air speed of

700 miles per hour (Mach 1.06) in his Bell Aviation X-1 plane. Three weeks later, he streaked to Mach 1.35; six years later, he flew at an incredible 1,612 miles per hour (Mach 2.44), putting to rest the myth of an impenetrable barrier. Yeager wrote in his autobiography:

THE FASTER I GOT, the smoother the ride. Suddenly, the Mach needle began to fluctuate. It went up to .965 Mach—then tipped right off the scale. I thought I was seeing things! We were flying supersonic! And it was as smooth as a baby's bottom: Grandma could be sitting up there sipping lemonade.

I was thunderstruck. After all the anxiety, breaking the sound barrier turned out to be a perfectly paved speedway. . . . I sat up there feeling kind of numb, but elated. After all the anticipation to achieve this moment, it really was a let-down. . . . The ughknown (*sic*) was a poke through Jello. Later on, I realized that this mission had to end in a let-down, because the real barrier wasn't in the sky, but in our knowledge and experience of supersonic flight.

Similar to Yeager's story is the account of Roger Bannister, the first man to break the four-minute mile. For years leading up to 1954, milers and track experts, even physicians, claimed that the four-minute barrier was unbreakable by a human being. When Bannister cracked it, a mental or psychological barrier was also broken. In the two years following Bannister's record-breaking run, forty-two people accomplished the same thing—a staggering number when you think that just two short years earlier it was "impossible" for anyone. Bannister did more than break the four-minute mile, he shattered the concept of human limitations. He changed our perception of reality. After that, breaking the four-minute mile was simply something for runners to shoot for, not something out there beyond our grasp.

· Valuing the Individual

I knew that I would need to overcome resistance to change within Toro. To do that, I wanted to involve all employees in the decisions regarding our future and how we would get there. I wanted our people to own our direction and to feel accountable for it, so I focused on the process of making the right decisions rather than on making decisions myself. I wanted the Toro Team to experience something John Naisbitt described in *Reinventing the Corporation*: "When you identify with your company's purpose, when you experience ownership in a shared vision, you find yourself doing your life's work instead of just doing time." Can you think of anything more dismal than "doing time"? Consider this passage from *In Search of Excellence* by Tom Peters and Bob Waterman:

> ARE THESE MEN AND WOMEN workers of the world? . . . What is it about that entrance way, those gates to the plant? . . . What is it that instantaneously makes a child out of a man? Moments before, he was a father, a husband, an owner of property, a voter, a lover, an adult. When he spoke at least some listened. Salesmen courted his favor. Insurance men appealed to his family responsibility and by chance the church sought his help. . . . But that was before he shuffled past the guard, climbed the steps, hung up his coat and took his place along the line.

For me, this is an extremely vivid image. What struck me was that the employees of Toro were those same people we had asked to make sacrifices and to become partners with us during the crisis of 1981, and who engaged in the long-term effort to turn Toro around. How could we not respect and value these men and women who kept Toro and our vision alive? None of our corporate goals could be met without the Toro people. If it weren't for them, there would be little reason for management to show up for work in the morning. Our stockholders would also be unhappy with our performance as a company. And many of those stockholders are Toro employees. If I weren't able to communicate to them the faith and vision I wanted them to share, there was going to be very little harvesting for any of us.

That's why, early on, we set a goal to break down the barriers that separated management and staff. We wanted our people to work together, to understand each other, and to value each other. That's one reason our management, i.e., our officers and directors, walk in the shoes of others by working on the assembly lines at each plant. It's good to remind ourselves that ultimately, we're all doing the same job. It's our way of doing something Tom Peters suggests, turning the plant (and the organizational chart) upside down. To weld and paint and bolt and pack and load lawn mowers, trimmers, and sprinkler heads from time to time is very enlightening, a humbling experience to management, and gratifying to the production workers. It helps us see that every person in our organization has tremendous gifts and potential, and their contribution isn't defined by their position on the organizational chart.

There are differences between seeding a golf course, with its expected result of perfectly manicured grass, and seeding a garden, where the result is less predictable. We learned through trial and error that different seeds produce different results. Different people exhibit unique strengths that have to be cultivated, and that's the leader's job. As a friend of mine pointed out, "With gardens, it ain't all beets." At Toro, management came to value this uniqueness in each of our people. Our management team took the beliefs we developed in conjunction with our Pride In Excellence culture, and wrote the following philosophy statement to reflect the worth and uniqueness of each employee:

WE BELIEVE the single most important factor that influences our success as a company is the Toro employee.

Therefore, it is our privilege and responsibility to create a culture and an environment that supports and encourages individuals at Toro to achieve their highest potential.

In order for employees to achieve their potential, we accept the responsibility to show by our actions that we care about them as individuals, understand their needs, recognize their talents, and support them in their efforts to grow and change. At the same time, all of us as employees must accept responsibility for our own performance and foster the environment that facilitates this accountability.

As a company, and as the people of Toro, we pledge to execute this philosophy genuinely and with excellence. By doing so, we believe that Toro will be most successful in meeting its overall corporate goals.

Toro's management team continually reviews and reinforces our employee philosophy, and since 1989 Toro managers have earned a significant part of their annual incentive award on the basis of their practice of this philosophy. Who are the judges of their performance? The judges are their subordinates and their peers. It works like this: Each year, our senior managers and their teams review those areas in the manager's behavior that inhibit the team members from quality work or obtaining their goals, and that are inconsistent with the employee philosophy. Three leadership objectives are agreed upon by the team, and initial ratings are fed back (confidentially, if desired) to the manager. During the year at least one interim review occurs, and at year-end final ratings and comments are collected from subordinates and peers. Thus an overall score and a subsequent incentive award are determined.

After we adopted this appraisal system and attached financial consequences, we began to see significant management behavior changes, and the Toro folks knew that the employee philosophy was more than mere words on a wall.

The Total Quality Barrier

Some barriers, such as a quality standard, can also pose a psychological barrier. We had to deal with a quality-standard barrier as we started to talk about "zero defects" because initially the head of Toro's parts business was at odds with the concept. He was terribly proud of his fill rate—the best in the industry at 98 percent, meaning that 98 percent of the time he delivered the order correctly and on time. It was a record to be proud of, without a doubt.

But I remember telling him, "The other side of the coin is that 2 percent of the time you're not satisfying the customer. If you have 75,000 orders to fill in a year, you'll end up late or incomplete on 1,500 of them. That's a lot of dissatisfied customers. What if you're one of the 2 percent? How do you feel about a 98 percent fill rate? You wouldn't care, because the parts department failed when it mattered to you."

He argued, "To get 100 percent, I'd have to keep so much inventory on hand, it wouldn't be economically prudent."

I said, "Larry Bird, former star player for the Boston Celtics, had a free-throw shooting average of 92 percent, the best in the NBA. In the 1990 season, he had a string of sixty-eight before he missed—that's awfully close to the record of seventy free throws. A 92 percent average means he could miss eight out of one hundred. Now, suppose he's getting to the end of his streak of sixty-eight, do you think he gets to the line and says to himself, 'It's okay to miss this one, and the next couple of times too, for that matter. I don't need to concentrate'?

"What if the game is on the line, and it's important that he makes it? To his customers (his coach, fellow players, the fans) it's probably never okay to miss one. I think Larry Bird expected to make it every time he was at the line. He didn't expect any defects. It didn't matter if he made 98 percent before, he still expected to make the shot. And if he ever missed two in a row in a game, he'd spend four hours the next day just practicing free throws. Having a defect or two wasn't acceptable to Larry Bird. He must have said to himself, 'It's not acceptable for me to miss, especially two in a row, and I'm going to prevent that from happening the next time.'"

As we talked, I defined zero defects as an attitude. "You're like Larry Bird," I told him. "He wasn't judged as *bad* when he missed, but he didn't accept a miss. And yet he and the team could live with it. The way I define zero defects is an attitude that allows for continuous betterment and enhances the possibility of planned perfection. In other words, if you say to yourself, 'It's okay not to satisfy a few or even 2 percent of our customers,' then it will be harder to get better and you'll probably never reach the ideal. But if you say, 'It's unacceptable to fail to satisfy 2 percent, or just two customers,' and you define ways to get better, that creates an environment in which you're always moving toward total satisfaction, and maybe even able to reach 100 percent."

We see few real business examples of 100 percent. Our management team went to Milliken & Company, the fabric manufacturer in

Spartanburg, South Carolina, to try and understand their approach to quality. At that time, they had one plant that had experienced zero defects for seven years—not one fabric defect in seven years. Eventually, perhaps, the plant will have a defect, and they'll have to start the count over again. But for a seven-year period they've had a perfect record. I think that's possible at Toro. It's not only possible, I believe it's also probable. But to reach zero defects, you have to plan for perfection.

The parts executive eventually became convinced. He finally accepted, even embraced the idea. Although he was a "real world" kind of guy, he came to believe that 98 percent just wasn't good enough and that the solution to reach 100 percent didn't necessarily mean loading the warehouse with inventory. He learned to attack the system and to find new or improved processes that would enable him to reach the ideal.

The Final Two Percent

When I went to the Crosby College of Quality in Winter Park, Florida, we talked about the concept of removing obstacles that prevent employees from executing quality in their jobs. When I returned to Toro, I was eager to use what I had learned, but I realized that I would need to model the process for others. To achieve total quality, you need to focus on what you're doing and how to do it better. I thought about how my being late to meetings kept others from achieving quality. I felt that if I made a concerted effort to be on time to meetings, using the total quality process approach, it would reinforce my commitment to quality in my job and to the whole initiative. I began tracking my on-time arrivals by circling the meetings for which I was late on the card I always carry around with me that outlines my meeting schedule. I did this for a few weeks so I could quantify the problem. I was shocked to find I experienced not 2 percent but 35 percent defects!

Since I'm a big believer in the rule, *what gets measured gets managed*, I set up an ongoing measuring system using my daily schedule cards. I returned them at the end of the work week with the tardy meetings marked; my secretary then quickly figured out my on-time percentage, and recorded it on a large histogram displayed on an easel. We put the easel outside my office so other employees could see my progress—or lack of it.

Charting progress against goals and displaying that progress for others to see are effective in changing behaviors. People become more focused and disciplined about progress because they don't want others to see the gap persisting. When I began doing it, it was rather embarrassing—until I began achieving a weekly rate of at least 90 percent! Seeing my own practices result in scores of 70 or 80 percent really motivated me to do better. Eventually, my focus and determination brought me up to 90 percent, but I soon realized I had plateaued and couldn't close the gap to 100 percent.

To get past the 90 percent level, my secretary and I began examining the processes involved in scheduling the meetings and the root causes for my tardiness. A little Pareto analysis (i.e., assembling the data in such a way to indicate the frequency of each problem cause), communication, and common sense led to some process changes, and I managed to get up to the high nineties consistently. I could even achieve a weekly rate of 100 percent—zero defects! Moreover, other managers became more serious about being on time and the meeting discipline in the entire company improved, leading to a good productivity gain.

While this was a seemingly small issue, it had a large impact on the organization. Sometimes it takes simple examples to demonstrate that ideas work in more complex situations too. The problem-solving procedure used here follows five basic steps:

1. Clearly identify the problem or situation.
2. Apply a quick and temporary fix while solving the core problem.
3. Identify root causes and new processes that help you reach your goal.
4. Take corrective action.

5. Evaluate and follow up to insure the proper solution is implemented.

Most of the time you never finish because, in this complex business world with ever-increasing customer requirements, meeting standards and goals requires constantly improving your systems. The process repeats itself over and over.

Personal Improvement

I see my own efforts as a link in the movement toward continuous improvement. Having that easel and the histogram outside my door personalized my approach to quality and put my personal work goals on public display. In part, it's my way of personalizing what Deming, Crosby, Juran, Taguchi, and the other quality masters are saying. For example, I always have some personal objectives for myself, things I believe will make me a better CEO and leader, such as those described below.

ROLE MODEL IMPROVEMENT

I always incorporate some practices in my daily work regimen that illustrate what I'm asking others to do, whether it's embracing our vision, improving quality, being a coach, initiating change, getting closer to the customer, or developing stronger teams. I typically gather feedback from employees about things that should be changed or enhanced, and then develop a plan to accomplish the changes that includes a way for me to track my progress.

This past year my goal was to improve my sense of spontaneity and humanness with our employees. During fiscal 1993, we were in a turnaround period and each employee could earn a recovery award if the company achieved its earnings-per-share target. It made sense to gather as a group for a monthly update on our progress, reviewing the period's financial results for each division and the success stories and efforts leading to the results. We called these meetings the "Coach's Huddle." At these twelve meetings, I donned various coach's uniforms—football, basketball, or baseball, depending upon the season—and played the role of the coach. It was awkward at first, but it got easier and more natural each time, and employees began to see me as more human.

CLARIFYING EXPECTATIONS OF AND FOR SUBORDINATES

I tend to want to cut through the preliminaries and go to the core of an issue. I don't have a lot of patience for extraneous material and analysis; I tend to tune out, having little time for all the detail. I believe most hour-long meetings can be synthesized down to twenty minutes, so I'm always looking for ways to separate the wheat from the chaff and get to the critical parts of the issue. I want twenty-minute executive summary presentations that are well organized and prepared. I'm trying to hone in more directly on the results or outcomes I expect from activities, so people know early on if they're on target or not.

DEALING WITH CONFLICT MORE OPENLY AND HONESTLY

I want to make sure everyone presents his or her real feelings and opinions, so I want to create an environment of trust. I want people to know that it's okay to disagree with me and others, and that their views are valued. I encourage everyone to seek the goodness in an idea even if it seems at first blush to be unworkable or off the mark.

DEMONSTRATING THE TOTAL QUALITY PROCESS

I try to use the total quality process in my daily interactions. For example, by communicating with management, employees, and customers anywhere and anytime—and by requiring other members of the management team to do the same—I'm attacking projects and coming to decisions using the total quality terms and process overtly. It's a slow process, but it builds and eventually mushrooms. If employees can't see the models and initiatives practiced by management, then they'll fade, and employees will return to their old behaviors.

PROVIDING MORE RECOGNITION OF EMPLOYEES AND TEAMS

I work with our total quality facilitators to bird-dog efforts (they see them all the time) that exemplify quality and drive out nonconformances. This gives me plenty of opportunities to recognize people who are working the system and getting results. This, I've found, is a built-in multiplier of positive energy.

EMPHASIZING EFFECTIVE AND TIMELY DECISION MAKING

Employees get frustrated with all the bureaucracy and the seemingly inordinate amount of time it takes to get things done in an organization. They tune out just as I do; they don't have the time either. Speed is key, and it gets more critical all the time. Decision making and product development alike need the sense of urgency that comes from the attitude that we can indeed create our own future. Taking too long to decide, waffling and backtracking on decisions made, and not obtaining team support all frustrate employees. Urgency is lost while energy is wasted. So make every attempt to accelerate the process and force outcomes, while still making clear that responsibility and accountability must be driven down the organization.

FOCUSING ON SIGNIFICANT SUCCESS FACTORS

I try to bring more focus onto the few significant success factors and goals that will transform the company. Focusing the entire organization repetitively and clearly on the company's goals has tremendous power, but it's still essential that people understand your expectations and know what you *don't* want.

MODELING AND ENCOURAGING CONTINUOUS PERSONAL BETTERMENT

I try to model continuous personal betterment and encourage others to adopt it as a working philosophy. I want people to understand that they can and should be working toward continuous personal betterment as well as day-to-day achievement of quality in their jobs—that we have a total quality process we're implementing at Toro and they're an important part of it. This is the most direct method we have of cutting down the cost of nonconformance.

Personal Responsibility for Results

Philip Crosby, at the Crosby College of Quality, told us that the cost of nonconformance at Toro is at least 10 percent of sales: in other words, almost $100 million. I didn't expect it to be that high, but I was sure it was big enough to warrant a massive attack on all fronts. The key to lowering that percentage in an environment that asks people to take personal responsibility for quality is to translate the $100 million into requirements for each person.

For example, within our two largest divisions we process over eleven hundred engineering change orders (ECOs) in a year. Many of these change orders are related to innovation changes, cost reductions, or compliance with new legislated requirements. However, 20 percent of these changes are due to mistakes: errors that shouldn't have happened in the first place. The cost to Toro is significant. We have a team in phase two of its quality project that has identified the preventable engineering change orders. The team has set goals and has established processes to reduce and eventually eliminate the preventable ECOs. The team is committed to helping reclaim that $100 million lost in waste and rework.

We have other continuous improvement projects in place. But only if we individualize the efforts of all four thousand employees will we be on our way to beating that $100 million. And the only way individuals will take personal responsibility for quality is if leaders set the example. By starting with my individual commitment to be on time, tracking my own incremental improvements, and demonstrating real concern for the individual, or whatever walk illustrates my talk, I can turn to our people and say, "You have to make personal goals for yourself; you have to work on those goals every day; your commitment has to be real; you have to be willing to make it public; and we're in this together."

As leaders demonstrate their commitment to quality, this attitude spreads and every individual assumes a high degree of personal responsibility for his/her job and for the overall success of the company. We deal with quality on an individual level. We trust that individuals will perform better if they look at their jobs, figure out what the obstacles to quality are, and then deal with those obstacles. By recording and tracking their progress, with the help of supervisors who are committed to coaching employees through the improvement process, individuals will perform better. And if each individual performs better, the organization will perform better.

If the organization is to make progress, *each individual has to identify a role and take responsibility for contributing to solutions.* If you have an attitude of continuous improvement and translate it into individual performance, you'll make incremental progress. Multiply that by all your employees, and you'll unleash enough potential to solve whatever problems your organization may face.

The ESOP Fable

Ownership is an important influence on behavior. One of my friends, a successful real estate broker, insists that when he drives by a house he can immediately tell by the condition of the house and the appearance of the lawn whether the property is occupied by owners or by renters. I believe the same is true of ownership in the workplace, which can come from having made a commitment to the mission and vision of the enterprise. In turn, ownership provides a platform, a foundation on which quality can be achieved. Ownership exudes a sense of pride; we normally want to preserve and improve what we own.

Employee ownership has been one of the elements of our culture shift, and the ESOP (employee stock ownership plan) has been a good move for Toro. I remember a *Business Week* article a few years ago that reported on companies that had created ESOPs to improve productivity. In actuality, the results were regrettably grim. They concluded that ESOPs did not do what they professed to do. This, and other stories like it, spread what I call the ESOP fable—the idea that you put an ESOP in place in order to increase employee productivity, with the result of little, if any, productivity gain.

In our experience, initiating an ESOP to increase productivity without a vigorous and supportive culture in place is putting the chicken before the egg, or perhaps more appropriately—attempting to harvest before seeding. Culture must come first. My advice: get the organizational environment right, establish genuine employee ownership in both the company and its vision for the future, and then institute a quality or productivity improvement initiative. In this way, a true sense of ownership will grow and become a reality and the company will benefit as well as the employees.

Cellular Management

Other nurturing methods also produce ever-increasing feelings of ownership. One method we use in some of our manufacturing facilities is called cellular management—building products in work cells. Instead of the old way, lots of people on the assembly line performing their individual functions and feeling detached from the final product, cellular management consists of large subunits and teams, each involved in and accountable for the production of the whole product. The more identifiable the component or product is with the customer or the end user, the greater is the cell's ability to focus on complete customer satisfaction.

When our customers visit our production facilities, they may talk to cell members about their experiences with the product and share their ideas on ways to make the product better. Cell members take on a new level of ownership of their product and their production unit. They identify with the product and respond with a great deal of pride to the performance of the product. The feeling of ownership and the recognition from customers engender a standard for quality, and in effect, change the attitudes of the employees and the team. The notion that quality comes from good, positive attitudes is reinforced. I believe that quality is 10 percent the result of skill, 10 percent the result of process, and 80 percent the result of attitude.

We have a cell at our production facility in Tomah, Wisconsin, that makes large fairway mowers. Another cell, whose team members have been together for many years, is responsible for riding greens mowers. When each cell completes a product, a cell member bolts a brass nameplate onto the product declaring that "This Parkmaster" or "This Greensmaster was made with pride by" and then the signatures of all the cell members are engraved on the nameplate.

The same esprit de corps and pride are going on today in our Riverside, California, facility, which produces sprinkler heads. The product is complex with nozzles, plastic gearing, seals, membranes, and other intricate small parts. Some time ago, the production employees each had a singular function in constructing the gear-driven sprinkler head. Today you're more apt to find employees around a large "lazy-Susan" table selecting components from the rotating tabletop and constructing complete sprinkler heads.

Cells have complete accountability for the total product; members talk at the end of the week about how they have performed against their goals and how to do better the next week. The team focus on customer requirements with a sense of ownership, accountability, and pride unleashes each cell's potential to achieve new heights of total quality and self-fulfillment.

Customers as Partners

Over the years, we've tried very hard (with fairly good results) to dissuade our distributors from taking on competitive products. Most of our competitors have not had the benefits of a partnership with their customers. Our forefathers had recognized the importance of singular distributor loyalty to Toro. When our independently owned distributors are 100 percent Toro, we are able to view the distributor as an extension of our company. Because we are able to partner with our distributors, they view Toro not just as a supplier but as part of the family.

Our many years of partnership have engendered this sense of family. I believe this was a key ingredient in our appeal to the distributors to become equity partners in the proposed acquisition of

Cushman-Ryan (see page 138). We have long believed that distributors who carry competitive lines eventually look at us as just another supplier, and we tend to look at them as another customer, with the attendant barriers to trust. Our survival depends on having a strong interdependency between Toro and our distributors, the breaking down of that barrier between supplier and customer.

Attempts to buy off employees or manipulate customers miss the mark. Insincerity buys you nothing. You'll find you're only "renting" the hearts and minds of the men and women who are your best chance to succeed. Anchor your efforts in building an environment that not only *allows* individual betterment, but also *demands* it each and every day. You'll see improvement, both along the line and in your bottom line. Every company has hard times at some point in its history and faces the need for recovery and rediscovery. The question is whether you, as a leader, are capable of breaking a few barriers, of achieving the final 2 percent, of empowering your people to move your company back to health and toward excellence. If you want to move beyond the plateau that seems to have you stalemated, try moving the power down through your organization. Work to create a genuinely empowering environment so that the men and women who work with you can rediscover in themselves and renew in the organization the entrepreneurial spirit that made your company successful in the first place.

CHAPTER ELEVEN

The Renewal and Conservation of Resources

Solving problems merely returns you to normalcy.
Creating opportunities moves you forward.
— ANONYMOUS

GENERALLY, MOST OF US in the United States experience the things in our world as plentiful and in rich supply. We can scarcely imagine what it must have been like for our parents (or grandparents) to live through the years of World War II and struggle through shortages of virtually every commodity we take for granted today.

For most of us, perhaps the only event in our lifetime that reflects our country "doing without" was the gasoline shortage in the 1970s. For the first time, many American consumers were threatened with a shortage and panic buying set in. Seemingly overnight, we faced long lines at the pumps and even some rationing as prices shot up. Many people took a stand, stating unequivocally that they wouldn't buy gasoline if the price reached a dollar a gallon. But it did, and we kept buying while supplies lasted. We continue to do so, with hardly a look backward, and twenty years later we once again view the supply of gasoline and petroleum products as plentiful and never ending.

I believe in applying conservation principles to all resources—human as well as capital and natural. It's ludicrous to develop employees only to waste or discard them without a second thought. The price of repeated turnover is very high; that's why Toro values its low turnover rate (less than 4 percent in 1993 and 1994). People are a valuable resource, well worth conserving. A leader must cultivate a talent for seeing and developing the potential in people, as well as in situations. Without that talent, resources begin to deteriorate in subtle ways, and before you know it, you've allowed a downward inertia to begin, and it becomes doubly hard to recover.

Five Percent at a Time

When deterioration occurs little by little, it's hard to detect. It's like periodically taking 5 percent of the chocolate out of a chocolate bar. Before you realize it, you no longer have a chocolate bar. You can do it once or even twice, and the consumer may not notice; but if you do it every month, eventually people will satisfy their sweet tooth another way.

When I worked for The Pillsbury Company as a marketing manager, one of my product-line responsibilities was refrigerated fruit turnovers and coffee cakes. The division management was always fighting for cost reduction, and my boss would say, "Why don't you take 5 percent of the cherries out of the cherry turnover?" Or "Suppose you take 5 percent of the apples out of the apple coffee cake?" So I would go to the research and development lab and have a batch of turnovers and coffee cakes made with the reduced formulation for comparative testing.

When the samples were made, we'd go to the company's in-house testing facility, where 120 people would taste both the current and new product and rate the two on a nine-point scale. The results would come back: 7.8 satisfaction for the existing product and 7.6 or

7.7 for the new. The difference would not be statistically significant, so we concluded that people couldn't tell the difference. We assumed it was safe to take out 5 percent of the fruit. Six months later, my boss would again say, "We need to reduce these costs! Take another 5 percent out."

We repeated the process, and again consumers couldn't tell the difference. Perhaps we even repeated this a third time. Now had we compared the third iteration with the original turnover, the difference would have been significant! We realized that we were quietly and slowly removing the quality from the product.

Unfortunately, we sometimes do the same thing to our people. Look at the cumulative impact of inhibiting or conflicting processes, policies, and programs on your people. Small things can fester and add up. It's the accumulation of the 5 percent each time that creates the stress and strain on your people and ultimately takes the quality out of them.

The Benefits of Retraining

While we at Toro don't execute well in all instances, we work to value every individual and try to do many things to build an environment supportive of the employee's personal growth. At the same time we enhance our environment for corporate growth. The biggest Achilles heel in our system is the very nature of our outdoor business. All of our products have seasons: in the absence of rain and sunshine, the grass doesn't grow and customers don't buy. This natural law works against an important concern of all employees—job security and job stability. Obviously, this seasonal nature of our business is disruptive to many employees and their families, and a constant issue for Toro management. Lack of rain and sunshine in the spring and summer can make matters much worse. Whatever the season or the weather, we're still responsible for the livelihood of our employees and their families.

We learned a lesson from Milliken & Company, the fabric company that was our model for zero defects. Milliken taught us that it's important to retrain and redeploy employees if you anticipate a slowdown leading to a temporary layoff. Management has the moral obligation to use or build the skills and abilities of those who would normally be laid off. Try to find ways to assign other tasks or create new ones for them—perhaps refurbishing machinery or improving facilities—something that will make them more productive in the future and provide employment during the layoff period, even if the work is only part time. After all, that's what you'd try to do with any other asset if its intended use was temporarily suspended.

We once had a problem with a large piece of commercial equipment that many golf courses were using, a problem that cropped up at the same time we anticipated laying off twenty-four people for a two-month period. We knew we had to send a team of technicians into the field to fix the equipment. The alternative was to recall the product, which would have been much more costly and time consuming. The golf course superintendents wanted their units repaired as soon as possible because this occurred during the playing season. Our solution was to train the twenty-four people who were to be laid off to repair the equipment, and to send them into the field to do just that. We trained them, gave them a travel allowance, and said, "Your job for the next two months is to work with our distributors in the affected territories to fix these machines. The local distributors will work with you to give you support."

By developing a way to repair the equipment in the field, we created a win-win proposition that combined both maintenance and conservation principles. The golf course managers appreciated having responsive, on-site repair of the equipment. The fact that Toro sent people into the field to repair the machines demonstrated our care for and commitment to the customer. The employees we reeducated were excited to have an opportunity to travel and to perform a new job. They completed their field work in eight weeks and returned, eager to share their experiences with their coworkers as the plant was getting back to normal production levels.

The situation also brought some unexpected benefits. "Boy," one technician said, "the stuff we're building back at the plant is the best. You should see it function out in the field." Another said,

"We've got great distributors. And you should have seen the golf course at Pebble Beach. The course superintendent showed me embankments and hills you'd have thought no piece of equipment could mow—but there it was, one of our Reelmasters." Some learned how important the Toro irrigation system was to the superintendents. The superintendents' positive feelings about Toro and our equipment gave our employees a sense of pride and gratification in their work. Their excitement was contagious; other employees picked up on it. Our people suddenly saw Toro as a creative company that valued them as individuals, as people who did more than stand at a punch press or metal bender for eight hours a day.

I was thrilled to hear how this experience energized these employees. And because it was an experience completely outside their regular job descriptions, it helped us avoid the tendency to categorize people in ways that ignore or deny their unique experiences, personalities, and motivations. We're often blind to the capabilities and desires of people who work in single-dimension jobs. We tend to think they can do just one task, and that limits our understanding and appreciation of them.

If we accompanied that same person outside the workplace, we might discover that he or she is a regular churchgoer, maybe even an elder in his or her church. Maybe she is on the board of directors of the local YMCA and headed the neighborhood fund-raiser last year. Or we might discover that he's a family man who's well-read about health care or K–12 education. There are more dimensions to a person's life than we ever suspect when he or she comes to work on Monday morning.

When you claim to value the individual, you have to do more than put your commitment in writing on the wall in the center of your building (as we do with our employee philosophy statement). You have to repeat it and repeat it. Jack Welch, CEO of General Electric, found that employees ask the same questions about company philosophy, values, and purpose over and over, even though they've heard it before. And so you have to tell them again, and more importantly, you have to practice it and practice it. If you claim to value employees and their input, you have to include them in your decision-making processes, believe their input is valuable, and respond to their ideas and feelings. Otherwise it's artificial, and employees can see right through you.

From Rhetoric to Reality

At one time we were seriously considering purchasing robotic welders. Like many other American firms under pressure from Japanese counterparts, we were constantly looking for ways to improve our competitiveness. We had some suitable applications, and the division management wanted to explore this more advanced welding technology. Since this suggestion meant a major departure from the status quo, it was met with the usual share of skepticism and disinterest.

We planned to attend a national manufacturing technology show to learn about the available options and then visit a few of the manufacturers in their own facilities for demonstration. We identified four manufacturers of robotic welders whose products were consistent with our needs. We decided the best evaluators of the various robots were our own welders since they knew more about welding than anyone else. Two of our welders, who were highly respected by their peers for their craftsmanship as well as their leadership, along with two of our engineers, were asked to visit the vendors of each robotic welder.

After visiting all four manufacturers, our selection team evaluated the quality of the welds produced by each robot, the ease of operation, and the cost-effectiveness of each machine. Not only were the welders (who were originally skeptics) won over by the robotic welders, they also agreed on which robot to purchase and, along with the engineers who accompanied them, made the recommendation to management. Management accepted the recommendation of our "experts," and a new robotic welder went on line.

The welders were surprised at our willingness to listen to them. Once we broke through the initial, predictable resistance to the idea of robotic welders, they were excited to become involved with the high-tech equipment. Since we were also sending them to school to learn to work with the new equipment, they saw it as an opportunity to renew old and develop new skills. And the truth of the matter was, we got a better robotic welder because of their involvement. After all, who knows more about welding than welders! Some time later, during a meeting with the production employees, I was asked by another welder when we would be buying more robotic welders because he wanted to work with one too!

We then applied the same process to purchasing forklift trucks. We involved maintenance employees and drivers in the selection of ten new trucks. Also, our parts pickers and clerks—the people most directly involved in filling customer parts orders—were instrumental in developing and selecting our small parts material handling system. These people know their stuff! Involve them to help you grow, and involve them to help them grow! Renewal and conservation—both are essential elements.

Project Ernie

Let me tell you about something we called "Project Ernie." By 1990, Ernie Joyner had worked for Toro for forty-eight years and had already passed his seventy-seventh birthday. (At eighty-two, one year older than our company, he's still going strong!) He had worked for the company longer than any other individual. And, of course, he didn't want to retire, but at seventy-seven it's hard to stand in the same place for eight hours a day. Still, an individual like Ernie is worth conserving.

One day our employee-involvement manager, the head of human resources, and the plant manager all came to my office and asked, "What do we do about Ernie?" Technology upgrades made the equipment Ernie had mastered obsolete. Although Ernie was a highly skilled machinist, the new computerized numerically controlled machines required a different kind of expertise. They didn't want him to retire, and I didn't either, but we all knew that a change had to be made. We started thinking, "What can we do with someone who has all that history with Toro?" We brainstormed various ideas about how to use this resource for the good of the company, including how we might create a whole new experience for Ernie. After some extensive training, he now operates sophisticated, computerized, numerically controlled equipment. A little effort on our part enabled us to keep Ernie as a productive member of the workforce. And, at age seventy-seven, it gave Ernie a whole new challenge and a new, refreshing exposure to some important kinds of work we do in the plant. Another example of renewal and conservation of resources.

We recently celebrated Ernie's birthday at our annual Quarter Century Club get-together (what Ernie and the rest of the members call the "Old Timers Club"). To be eligible, you have to have been with Toro for twenty-five years or more. Even if you're retired, you're still a member of the Old Timers Club. In years past, our gatherings have included a Minnesota Twins baseball game, and more recently, dinner and a play at a popular local theater. Between dinner and the play, a few of the Old Timers gave short speeches. In addition to celebrating Ernie's seventy-seventh birthday and his service to Toro, we recognized several others who were celebrating their fortieth and forty-fifth anniversaries with Toro. I'm always amazed at how many there are!

One Old Timer, Dale Sohns, couldn't be there that evening. He was in the hospital, scheduled for a heart transplant. We videotaped the program for Dale, just to include him in the festivities. Everyone got together for a group shot to wave and say hello to Dale. It was a way of preserving our heritage—a way of recognizing who and what we are—an act of conservation telling people they're important.

Beyond Maintenance

I see enrichment as an important part of renewing and conserving resources—a deeper dimension of improvement. As I wrote earlier, I believe that every person possesses great potential. And I believe that one of management's roles is to continually invest in people, to go beyond maintenance to beautification—not just making an individual more productive for the company, but also enriching people's lives and helping them to become better at whatever they want to become. Different managers will do this in different ways. There are, after all, many styles and systems for keeping people green and growing.

Years ago, when quality circles were becoming popular, we were beginning an employee involvement process in our plants. Our motivation was to get the people closest to the problems to solve them as they were best equipped to deal with the facts. Supervisors could assist by providing problem-solving techniques and information on the expense implications of the solutions. They could also find resources as needed outside the quality circle.

I once read an article from our Minneapolis newspaper about how quality circles had become widespread in one of our large local companies. In the article, a human resources manager answered the question, "Why do you have quality circles?" by saying, "Because it makes the employees feel good." I was shocked and dismayed, and I wondered how long that initiative would last. That was not a compelling or sustainable reason for quality circles. Employees eventually see through "involvement to make one feel good" as superficial and a form of manipulation. You really have to believe those employees can provide valuable input when you ask for it. Otherwise, it's lip service and will eventually backfire.

You can't get a good team effort from people who are being manipulated, and you can't expect men or women you're engaging superficially to reach their potential. Why should they? To benefit you? People who are manipulated become resentful and embittered; you'll never know the full worth of their contributions if your managerial style limits their willingness and ability to express themselves and develop their potential. Poor eyes limit your sight; poor vision limits your deeds.

A leader is a catalyst who helps people become more valuable by enriching their lives and helping them reach their potential. A leader encourages new growth that will result in better performance in a person who is then more whole. A leader identifies raw talents and explores creative ways to expand and apply them. That's why, at Toro, we might take a person out of human resources or information systems and put that person in charge of a division, or move a person out of product assembly in a plant and make him a total-quality facilitator. We might take a person out of service and put that person in charge of marketing, or take an engineer and put her in sales.

These are smart and imaginative people. They are human beings who have unique strengths, talents, and skills to offer. If you're willing to take some risks, empower them, and give them guidance and coaching, they will grow, bloom, and flower. If you want to build a community in your workplace—more than just a collection of people—give individuals something to reach for, help them make it happen, and expect that they will do it. I see my job as coaching and serving those with whom I work and fostering their growth. If you believe a person is unique, with great potential, you're ready to see that person rise to new heights.

I think leaders cultivate an eye for people with promise. Agreed, it's hard to see potential in some people. I remind myself that when you start measuring people, you have to measure them right. Make sure you have taken into account the hills and valleys they have traveled before they arrived at their current destination. Some people rise from the bottom or middle of an organization because of their educational backgrounds, their ambition, or their personalities. But these people aren't so different from those who move up more slowly, although our symbols of power and importance imply otherwise. Virtually everyone in an organization has mental aptitude, and everyone has unique experiences that make up their own wisdom and perspective. Our mental capacities are not all that different. A good mind coupled with unique experiences means a person has a great deal to offer. The NAACP slogan, "A mind is a terrible thing to waste," applies as much to the adults in our organizations as it does to students in our schools. There's not a person at Toro from whom I can't learn something. My challenge is to be more available, to spend more time with employees, so I can learn from each one of them.

Jogging is one of my passions. Rarely do I come home from the office without some issue on my mind. So when I'm out on a run, I invariably massage the issue six ways to Sunday. I review everyone's point of view and options; I try to understand why that person said what he or she did, why he or she held that particular point of view, what was good about it, and how it might be enhanced if we'd give it a chance. I sometimes come back to work the next day with a different opinion. When you give people a chance, they'll sprout roots in new directions and spawn new growth. It happens best when you preserve their existing roots, respect their value, and preserve their dignity.

Strength through Renewal

When we hire new employees, I invite them to my office for lunch or coffee and cookies. People come from companies of all sizes, but most come from similar work situations. They have lots of ideas they've brought from their previous experience that might have application to their new job. They often comment that they don't know what works here, what's been tried, or how to best make suggestions that will be listened to.

I tell them, "What you don't know is your strength. You're coming into this company and you don't know any better than to suggest ideas that we may have tried already, or ideas that our people would tend to dismiss by saying, 'Well, maybe that was good where you came from, but it won't work here.' The challenge to all of you is to see your lack of familiarity as a strength. Press us to look at things in new ways. You are our best paradigm shifters. Those who have worked here for ten, twenty, or more years are terribly valuable to us, but they're less likely to look at an old problem in a new way. You 'new hires' have that opportunity, but make it your responsibility too. Realize that you're different, and don't be so hasty to conform and become homogeneous. Be a beacon. Be a light. Dare to ask, 'Why are things done this way? Have you ever thought of doing it this other way?' Show us a new and better way. Persevere and don't let your ideas be discarded so easily."

By recognizing the value in the differences new people bring to our organization, we embrace an opportunity to renew ourselves.

Without renewal, we degenerate, sit idle, and lose our edge; we plateau and lose our momentum. How, then, do we hone the edge and keep the blade of our enterprises sharp? How then do we renew and conserve our resources? Empower and trust. Take a few risks. Dare to be an example to others. Respect others and earn respect yourself. Have a vision and share it. Promote a team mentality. Trust people, don't control them. Put people power to work. Know yourself. Experiment. Support others. Be honest. Involve others in what you want to achieve. Give them ownership. Eliminate whatever roadblocks you can. Listen. Encourage a healthy exchange of ideas. Care and coach. If you do these things, you can't help but renew and conserve your resources for their best uses.

Every Day Is Earth Day

Because Toro is an environmental company, we believe that every day is Earth Day. I often wonder how much people really care (the kind of care that leads to action and changed behavior) about the environment as a whole, about conservation of resources, about the reduction and even recycling of waste. I know everyone cares about preserving our air and natural beauties. As we made the transition from a lawn mower company to an outdoor environmental company, I came to realize how vital it is that we not only care, but that we put that caring into our products and our actions. How can we state, for example, that we are an environmentally concerned company if our actions don't back it up? To back up our convictions, more and more of our products are designed and marketed for environmental enhancement. Some examples are water-conserving irrigation systems, moisture sensors, soil-conserving and decompaction equipment, water aerifiers, recycling lawn mowers, composters for people who want to collect their grass clippings, and probiotic (life-enhancing) fertilizers.

We're working, too, to create ways for employees to participate in protecting the environment. For example, we have recycling programs at all our locations. The money earned from recycling efforts at our corporate headquarters goes to fund a raptor center, a society for the preservation of eagles, hawks, and other endangered avian species. On one of our annual employee celebration days, the raptor center brought one of its eagles to Toro. How fitting it was to award our top achieving employees their "Circle of Excellence" bronze sculptured eagles in the presence of a magnificent live eagle!

At Toro we think more today about conserving our natural resources. Toro is in the business of preserving, maintaining, and beautifying our natural resources, whether it's grass or soil or water. We try to make these things more beneficial for all humankind. For us, environmental concern isn't just over broad issues such as the diminishing ozone layer, the elimination of rain forests, water and air pollution, or some macro-trend that politicians argue about. Concern for the environment also relates to green trees or a well-maintained lawn and shrubs outside your front door. For most homeowners, environmentalism is a desire to live in their own healthy, green, and beautiful micro-worlds. In that sense, Toro has been in the business of beautifying, maintaining, and enhancing the environment ever since it began in 1914. And over the years, our environmental consciousness has increased with need, knowledge, and mission.

Each of us has the opportunity and responsibility to contribute positively to the environment by taking care of our own real estate and our personal possessions (even if we're only "renting") and by promoting environmental awareness in general. Use less, conserve, recycle, clean up, leave things better than when you found them, and you'll benefit from everything in your environment. An environmentally conscious lifestyle will add to your sense of self-fulfillment, and you'll receive positive feedback that will make you want to contribute more.

Healthy Working and Living Environments

There are other types of environmental pollution also, such as somebody literally blowing smoke in your face. That's a type of pollution we have tried to eliminate at Toro, to the relief of most of our people and the discomfort of a few. We still have a small group who smoke; we have found ways to allow them to smoke in outdoor areas so that our facilities are totally smoke-free.

This didn't happen all at once. Initially, we banned smoking in individual offices, at work stations, and in rest rooms; we provided a section of the cafeteria for smokers during coffee breaks and lunch. We installed large-capacity air-intake devices in the cafeteria ceiling that evacuated the smoke-filled air. As another intermediate step, we provided the smokers an inside area, a room for coffee breaks. We eventually eliminated indoor smoking entirely. Through this process, we tried to take into consideration that our smokers were valuable employees too. For example, these phased plans, based on broad surveys to quantify opinions and attitudes, were communicated up front to employees. And all during this process, we offered various smoking-cessation programs for smokers who wanted to cut down or eliminate their smoking habit. Since we knew 20 percent of our office population were smokers, we recognized that the problem and the solution were important to all of us. The number of employees who smoke today is far less than the original 20 percent, and while they have been inconvenienced, I believe they understood and appreciated the process.

Unlike when the environmental movement began in the late sixties, people today are more sensitive and responsive to environmental issues because of personal experience with the consequences of irresponsibility, whether it is the effects of passive smoke or landfill waste. Living and working environments that are clean and green are part of the Toro vision, and it would be inconsistent not to be environmentally proactive in our own corporate house.

As I've mentioned, I have a passion for white-water rafting trips. The physical challenge, the confrontation with nature, the grandiose scenery, all inspire and refresh me. I also love the pristine setting—the sense of nature in its purity, seemingly untouched by human hands, there to partake of, enjoy, and appreciate. There is no sense of pollution. You can watch the satellites move across the sky and a rare shooting star fall through the clear night air; you can camp in unblemished forests along rivers with pure, white, sandy beaches;

you can drink from the pure river water of the Salmon's Middle Fork River in Idaho. Such surroundings are so revitalizing because the norm in much of our world is contamination and pollution. It makes me want to return to the grass roots, to earlier times, and to nature.

I worry when I see what's happening in our world. I think that a green and clean world has the power to call us back to some of the deeper values, to an earlier moral consciousness that we in many ways have lost—a moral consciousness that tells us to do something because it's the right thing to do, that tells us to solve our own problems face-to-face, not through courts and lawyers that prey upon our sense of "what's in it for me." Just as we're losing the sense that moral consciousness guides our behavior, we may also be in danger of losing this clean and green world. At Toro, it's natural to work to preserve and enrich these values and the world they reflect; these are the things we take seriously.

A Corporate Ecosystem

An organization, like an ecosystem, consists of living, breathing organisms—accountants, engineers, customers, and suppliers who all work together to sustain life—just as trees, grass, and wildlife work together to sustain life. Growth occurs in a corporate ecosystem just as the growth of trees and plants occurs in nature. As a leader, you have a role to preserve and nourish that growth. The best way to do that—the only way to do it long term—is by conserving, beautifying, and enriching your resources each and every day.

If we don't do something about all the pollution facing us, we're going to die. All of us. The issue isn't about the survival of the planet Earth. Earth will survive humankind. The question is, will humankind survive itself? The enormity of that question prevents many of us from comprehending it. The task seems so huge and complex that a sense of futility stymies us, prevents us from doing tangible things with clearly visible results.

Still, each one of us can and must do something. We have to if we're to survive. This is true whether you're talking about creating a green environment or an empowering, supportive workplace. The environmental solutions require major changes and intervention by big players, but they also require a concerted effort by individuals. The challenge is to find individual contributions that each of us feels is worth the effort, especially when the immediate results are not so clear. For example, the collective goals of highway safety and energy conservation happen naturally when more people adhere to the fifty-five-mile-per-hour speed limit. When we do our individual part to preserve our natural resources and maintain a healthy natural environment, we meet our collective goals.

One could argue that most individual efforts are not quantitatively significant. But employees need to see that they are part of a massive wave of momentum and team force that could lead to success. Each needs to see others on the team actively participating and to hear the multitude of success stories that abound. For example, to achieve a massive turnaround in one year (from a nearly two dollar loss-per-share to a one dollar earnings-per-share in 1993), we had to enlist the effort of every employee. We not only had to translate the goal of one dollar earnings-per-share into specific contributions everyone could understand, but we also had to show how everyone's job affected our company's earnings.

To illustrate this point, I told a story at an all-employee meeting about a basketball game I played while in high school. I was not a starter, but our team was strong and highly ranked in the state of Florida. This game against Lakeland High School was a tournament game, so it was important. We were favored to win, but from the very outset we made enough mental errors to keep the score close. It seemed like our five starters were just not ready to play, so in frustration the coach began to substitute early in the second half. I played much of the last two quarters as a forward.

The score remained fairly even throughout, and with thirty seconds left, we were up by one, seventy-one to seventy. We had possession so it was just a matter of running out the clock. But an errant pass out of bounds turned the ball over to Lakeland. Lakeland brought the ball downcourt setting up for one last play. As it turned out, one of the guards took a long shot from the left side of the key.

I was in the rebounding position on the right and could see that the shot was too long, and that the ball would sail right over the rim. Having gained good position, I stepped forward to catch the ball.

What I didn't figure on was the ball hitting the lower right side of the backboard and bouncing back over my head into the hands of a Lakeland player who, before I realized what had happened, scored an easy layup behind my back. The buzzer sounded the end of the game; Lakeland won seventy-two to seventy-one. Well, the coach was livid and lit into me in a way that would make a sailor blush. I felt badly and fully realized that had I anticipated the backboard bounce, we would have won. But when he said the loss was all my fault, I fought back, at least in my mind. I couldn't help but think about the dribbling off knees, the missed layups, the walks, intercepted passes, and so forth by my teammates, any of which could have made the difference in winning or losing. My mistake was the most obvious, but no more critical than a host of others. It was true, however, that my little missed rebound made a big difference.

My point to the employees was that we all "make plays" throughout the year that, though seemingly insignificant at the time, could be very important in the end. And if we concentrate on excellence throughout the year we might avoid the need for heroics in the final month when we realize we're behind plan. If the goal is one dollar earnings-per-share, each can contribute. I wanted each employee to realize that his or her effort or work could mean the difference between ninety-nine cents and a dollar—in a sense, between winning and losing.

Joel Barker, a popular futurist, presents a film that shows the plight of starfish when the tide subsides. Washed up on the shore when the tide is in, the starfish are left to die on the sand. In the film, a jogger passes a boy throwing the starfish back into the sea, one by one. With so many dormant starfish, this appears futile to the jogger. He stops to ask the boy, "Why do it? It won't make a difference." The boy retorts, referring to the starfish he's pitching back into the water, "It does to this one!" It *does* make a difference, and each of us *do* make a difference.

The same principle is true in facing the problem of the environment. We all want the same thing—clean air, clean water, and green landscapes—but you need an engaging process and galvanizing vision in which to proactively enroll people. This is one of the benefits of our environmental mission—it purposefully galvanizes the organization toward a goal in which everyone can believe. But it only begins there. Setting and communicating a goal can mobilize the workforce toward an end, but unless there's a process to keep the troops marching in unison toward the goal, the odds of making it are low. People have to understand their role and worth, feel a part of the team that collectively and visibly makes a difference, and then be able to observe their team members actively working at it. Your chances are then much better for success.

If you personally embody the sense that you want to be a part of the solution and not the problem, this spirit can translate to your work and your everyday living. As a leader, you can call upon that spirit in yourself and in your people to work toward a world where the air is clean and the trees bud in the spring—and even bear fruit.

CHAPTER TWELVE

Creating the Future

We become what we choose.
— ANONYMOUS

WHY DO WE OFTEN FEAR competition and discipline when it's exactly what we need to move us forward? It's when we have to "do or die" that we get back to the basics, gear up, and move toward the future. We tend to get complacent, even apathetic, when times are good. In tough times, especially crises, we redefine and streamline ourselves; we retarget our goals with new energy and purpose.

The basic strategic choice in today's global arena is between administering what we have and creating what we need. The former is a hope to survive; the latter is a strategy to win. Today, there's no place for a "just renting" mentality or a business philosophy of "let's administer what we have." When competition intensifies, people and organizations have to choose a new paradigm and become more proactive, more innovative, and more customer responsive.

Sears realized in the late eighties that its strategy of administering what it had would no longer work; it knew it had to change. Its battle cry became: "Let's create what we need." It was a change both in attitude and in strategy. It was already too late for Sears to keep upstart Wal-Mart, who was about to pass Sears in retail sales, at bay. Sears, with its many layers of management symbolized by a monolithic office tower, went from dominance to floundering, while Wal-Mart, with few layers of management, experienced 6,000 percent growth in ten years, a sales increase from $400 million to $25 billion.

Many American companies spent a great deal of the eighties implementing and fine-tuning a survival plan, but they never moved beyond it. The decade was characterized by a focus on business fundamentals such as quality, culture, innovation, and operations excellence. But the survival mentality is not enough to succeed today; in fact, it might mean sure death. To put it another way, if your flight to Moscow from San Francisco is off course by only 1 percent, you'll land near Beijing! "Almost right" is becoming more unacceptable every day.

In the future we must create what we need if we plan to win. This strategy requires a more proactive approach, better use of technology, and new leadership with new skills, attitudes, and attributes. "We want to learn to love change," says Tom Peters, "because change will be omnipresent." At Toro, we began an effort toward world-class manufacturing by focusing on product quality, cost effectiveness, and just-in-time delivery to customers. This led to a world-class business with a focus on total quality, productivity, and customer satisfaction.

Five Elements of a Winning Strategy

As I've thought about what a winning game plan is, I've concluded there are five essential elements: vision, focus, quality, environment, and passion. Let's consider each.

VISION

The first order of business is to establish, communicate, and incorporate into the organization's life a well-defined vision that's understood and embraced by all. Our vision at Toro is to become a trusting and valuing organization, and to protect and preserve the outdoor environment, to make the landscapes "green," healthy and safe with superior quality, innovative and environmentally-sound products, services and systems. We also want to maintain market leadership, have consistent earnings growth, and strengthen our competitive position. Our vision at Toro has been embodied within a culture called Pride In Excellence, and we achieve that vision through our employees, our field players. Lou Holtz said, "Care for your players and staff; trust them, and the wins will come."

Ask yourself, "Do I have a vision? Is it written down? Can I recite it? Does it produce a plan to win or a plan to survive?" Then test the effectiveness of your communications. See if others can recite it. Ask various levels within the organization. You might be surprised at the answers, even from your top managers. Lastly, the acid test is how you and the rest of your leadership team incorporate the vision into your daily work routine. Are you "walking your talk," and do others perceive that you do? Because if they don't, your vision is just a piece of paper, a statement on the wall, and not "owned" by those in the organization.

FOCUS

Decide what's really important; define the key factors for success and your key business values; put first things first. For the past decade, Toro has had a focus on organizational climate. In addition, our focus on innovative product leadership for superior customer satisfaction, and passionate and superb customer service will carry us through the nineties.

Learn to think things through. This will prevent you from reacting prematurely and enable you to act appropriately, anticipating the future. Only a few things can be done well at any one time; if your focus is too broad you may miss make-or-break issues. As you narrow your focus to the most critical success factors, it may also be beneficial to clarify the minor issues, even the issues you are eliminating. People need to know not only what's expected of them, but also what's not. In the complexity of today's business environment, tenacious focus is critical. You can't afford time-consuming efforts on marginal endeavors.

QUALITY

With the advent of total quality management, quality was defined as a discipline *to do the right things right the first time.* Since then, the definition has become very specific to meeting customer requirements. If quality is what you're after, you'll find it can't be achieved without defining it. Conformance to requirements must then be demanded in all areas, including customer service, billing response, safety, valuing others, inventory turn, number of defects, and number of problems identified and solved.

While your definition must allow you to measure everyone's performance, it has to do more than tell you if you've met your objectives. Ideally, your adherence to quality will be a source of pride for everyone—labor, management, sales crew, and customer. I was thrilled, for example, when a friend told me that the Toro brand name is seen as the ultimate in his neighborhood. Owning a Toro in his neighborhood meant he had arrived. This customer-imposed expectation of excellence is something to be celebrated and something to be enjoyed with pride.

Adherence to quality is everyone's responsibility, from the secretary who sets a personal goal to input data for twenty-two purchase orders a day instead of the twenty she's been assigned, to the operator of the robotic welder on the line whose goal is 10 percent more throughput, to the members of the design team planning yet another improvement for an already successful product, to the parts manager who's shooting for a 100 percent fill rate. As the backbone of most systems, measuring and tracking tell us if our efforts are working and to what extent. Accountability in business is like a scoreboard in a football game. It allows us to focus on continuous betterment, but we have to be sure we know what we're measuring before we can decide if we're winning.

Delivering what your business dictates is important, but it must be defined in the customer's terms not yours. I recall visiting an automatic car wash that posted 6 p.m. as its closing time. When I pulled in, my car clock (which is usually a bit ahead) showed 5:58 p.m. There were three cars in line, but the operator wouldn't sell me a token. He stood there resolutely, shaking his head slowly and repeatedly at my explanation that I'd come a long way, and so on. His mental scoreboard showed 6 p.m. That's what his measuring stick was, not how many cars were washed that day, not profit made, not customer service, but the arrival in his mind of 6 p.m.

Roger Milliken, chairman and CEO of Milliken & Company, found that scoreboards provide great encouragement to employees to compete to win. Then too, Milliken & Company faced a unique situation. The focus throughout the organization was on betterment; the employees' approach (based upon the Toyota model) was to measure against a goal and then display their progress on a scoreboard— not just the number of problems *solved* but the number of quality inhibitors *identified*. Their error-cause removal system was prompted by each employee seeking out quality problems (things that prevented them from consistently achieving superior quality) and immediately reporting to their supervisor those problems they couldn't fix without support and help. Charts were maintained in each department to compare actual problems identified against monthly targets.

Milliken's philosophy has been to create an environment where problem identification is encouraged so that the organization can systematically eliminate every obstacle to quality. Measuring the number of reported problems is a key part of the process. Normally, people are reluctant to speak up about problems because they may believe that others feel the problems are inconsequential, or that they might be viewed as complainers, or that management wouldn't do anything about it anyway. At Milliken, problems are eliminated with proper follow-up and resolution within seventy-two hours. This process has yielded dramatic results. Over time, errors have been significantly reduced, and one plant ran a record seven years with zero defects. Quality means a process for identifying and eradicating defects and customer dissatisfaction, with a universal attitude of improving the process all the time.

ENVIRONMENT

The leader's values, philosophy, and behavior establish the corporate environment. I believe there are six dynamic leadership attributes that are essential for building the proper environment:

- Anticipate and respond to the future.
- Live your vision.
- Give power away.
- Create an environment for personal growth.
- Champion positive change.
- Integrate results and relationships.

By using these processes, servant leaders are able to transform organizations.

PASSION

Develop a passion to do the right things and then do them. Your actions must be overt, constant, genuine, tenacious, and comprehensive. The standards you adhere to must be the natural outgrowth of your philosophy and your personal value system. The message you communicate to your workers and to your customers can be neither mixed nor vague. You must genuinely believe in your philosophy and live according to that philosophy. You have to be more than consistent; you have to be passionate in your commitment. If not, you're destined to fail. You must communicate your expectations clearly and repeatedly, and provide continuous feedback on whether or not people are measuring up to those expectations and standards. When people see and feel your passion, it will mobilize and motivate them.

What Is Your Legacy?

Years ago, when I trained with thirty other adults to become a lay teacher of the Old and New Testaments in my church, our minister invited a Jewish rabbi to talk to our class one evening. As he began talking to us, the rabbi got onto the topic of the purpose of life. This was a rather esoteric subject, and most of us had fairly hazy views, if any, for our own selves. He pressed us by asking directly, "What's the purpose of your life? Why are you here?"

Some in the class described themselves as just taking one day at a time. Others felt life was too complex and hectic to warrant such consideration. Many hadn't even thought about their personal mission or purpose on this earth. And then there were those who felt they had no purpose—at least not that they could identify and put into words.

The rabbi said, "How many of you remember your grandfather? If you do, raise your hand." Almost everyone did and could cite a number of memories and characteristics about their grandfathers. Then he asked us how many could recall our great-grandfather. "Can you recall some of his traits?" Only a very few said, "Sure, I remember him." Then, "What about your great-great-grandfather?" the rabbi asked. "How many of you remember your great-great-grandfather?" Nobody, of course, did. "How many of you remember his name?" he asked. "The color of his eyes? Anything about his life?" We were all silent.

"All right," he said. "Now, let's move this forward. Suppose your grandchildren were in this room and they were your age, and I asked them the same questions about you. How many of them would remember you? Most of them would, of course. How about your great-grandchildren? Will they be able to remember you? Perhaps a few. And your great-great-grandchildren? Will they remember you? Will they remember your name, the color of your eyes, what you did?" The stark reality of it is that they won't. We will be gone years before they are born.

We realized that, of course, from our own experience. It is the way of the world. In four generations, our immediate families—

those who are closest to us—will likely have forgotten all about us. In just four generations we will cease even to be memories. Oh, there may be some traces of us they'll be able to find—letters, a memento, a fading photograph filed away in a drawer or on a shelf somewhere. Our great-great-grandchildren, however, will have absolutely no idea who we were. And if they don't remember, no one else will either.

"So what do you think about that?" the rabbi then asked. For me, it was a pretty sobering thought. It raised such questions in my mind as, "What *is* the purpose of my life? If I'll mean nothing at all to those just four generations ahead, why am I here today?"

The rabbi's answer was that we are all here to lead lives of purpose, and the purpose of life is to serve God and to serve humankind, however we choose to do so. He urged us to start some things of enduring value. Making long-term investments, such as protecting the environment, was probably worth our time and effort, he pointed out. No one is going to remember you as an individual in four generations, but they might well remember something you began, something you nurtured for someone else to foster, especially if our own families experience the benefits and results in their own lives.

Betty J. Eadie provides another good answer. In her account of her near-death experience and its aftermath, *Embraced by the Light,* she says, "We are here to help each other, care for each other, to understand, forgive, and serve one another."

I'm satisfied today that we have a definite momentum in the right direction at Toro, but I still ponder the rabbi's question. Like blades of grass, ten billion souls may occupy the world today, but who will be remembered in four generations? We grow and flourish like wild flowers; then the wind blows cold from the north, and the flowers are gone. Yet some of the wild flowers' seeds are scattered by that same wind, and some of them find soil that's ready to receive them, sun to warm them, and rain to nourish their growth.

At Toro, some of the seeds we've planted will come to fruition long after most of us are gone. Eventually, though, they'll bear fruit, and through generations there will still be people to benefit from our efforts. Plant a few seeds and a small crop will be harvested. Plant many seeds and you'll get a large crop. For most of us, it's the planting, not the harvesting, that's important, because in the planting we discover ourselves and our destiny as we move toward the future.

Seeds of Faith

In sports they say you're never as good as you think you are when you're winning, and never as bad as you think you are when you're losing. I think the same applies to business. In 1980, Toro's forward momentum was threatened. For a period of time, we had failed to recognize the interdependencies between Toro and our distributors and our suppliers. We hadn't seen the need to create prevention systems, so we merely reacted to situations rather than anticipate them. We hadn't been "sharpening the saw," and we didn't realize how important it was to do that. All of this meant that when the areas outside our control turned sour—such as the weather—we didn't have the internal strength, teamwork, trust, or incentive to overcome the problems we faced.

In recent years, much has changed, and because of those changes we face the future with excitement and confidence. We are stakeholders in a shared future, prepared to do whatever we need to do to overcome the problems we face. As we moved through the decade of the eighties, we learned to work as a team with our suppliers and our distributors, to develop solutions and solve problems.

In December 1986 we bought Wheel Horse, a lawn and garden tractor manufacturer with a direct dealer distribution system. In the past, we would have "Toroized" it immediately—changed all of the systems, integrated, consolidated, and amalgamated, until it emerged as another Toro product line. We'd have eliminated the Wheel Horse name, its direct distribution, its customer service ethic, and the product values that made the tractors Wheel Horse.

Instead, we took advantage of the potential synergies. While our Toro riding mowers had been growing nicely and our rear engine rider had been rated number one by *Consumer Reports*, the Wheel Horse people were the tractor experts. Our goal was to bring the stronger Toro brand name to the Wheel Horse product line, to integrate the two riding lines, utilize Wheel Horse's direct distribution, and gradually merge the best of each. Wheel Horse was very profitable, and we knew Wheel Horse was doing some good things, so in 1987 and 1988 we let Wheel Horse stand alone, to observe, understand, and learn its uniqueness and values.

Wheel Horse had an automotive marketing mentality, and while its styling was not contemporary, it did have a superior paint system that resulted in a glossier and richer red than Toro's traditional candy apple red. We displayed the Toro rider next to a Toro unit painted Wheel Horse red and asked our employees, "Which has a higher quality appearance?" Almost 100 percent preferred the Wheel Horse red. Over time, we changed all our Toro-brand products to the Wheel Horse red.

In addition to this visible element they brought to us, we also admired the fact that Wheel Horse had a dealer image as "easy to do business with." Its whole approach in dealing with customers was "Let's make it easy." Customers would say, "I like doing business with them because it's simple, it's clean, and it's quick. If I call customer service, I get an answer fast. I might not like the answer, but it's clear and it's now. And if I need a part, I get it quickly. If I have a problem, it gets solved. If I need to write an order, it's really easy to do."

One of Wheel Horse's main competitors in premium garden tractors is Honda, and Honda has a very complicated distribution system. It is telephone and computer driven—sophisticated, but according to many dealers not simple and easy, nor perceived as responsive. Learning computer systems, filling out a myriad of forms, plodding through a maze of corporate red tape, adhering to unclear policies and procedures, all are the opposite of the "easy-to-do-business-with" style that characterized Wheel Horse. Dealers, hardware store operators, lawn and garden centers, and outdoor power equipment shop owners are grassroots entrepreneurs struggling to make money, and many resist adapting their businesses to respond to the high-technology age. They like personal relationships, quick access to people with answers, and suppliers who can empathize with their concerns. Wheel Horse's style built loyal and strong long-term relationships with its dealers.

We wanted to maintain Wheel Horse's way of doing business and being responsive to its dealers, but use the Toro consumer equipment distributors as a sales agent force, which maintained a direct-selling structure for sales to these tractor dealers. We also wanted to incorporate Toro as the overall brand for advertising purposes, but use Wheel Horse's strong trade name to designate a riding mower category brand. By merging the strengths from the two branded businesses, we could provide new business for our distributors, still maintaining the selling structure, competitiveness, and customer responsiveness that made Wheel Horse successful. The added business for our distributors was also key to help facilitate some restructuring moves we felt were going to be necessary in the near future.

The Wheel Horse distribution system of direct selling, combined with using distributors as commissioned sales agents instead of using Wheel Horse's direct sales force, created a positive outcome for both parties. This was a significant cultural change for Toro, but it allowed us to recognize the Wheel Horse people for their contributions and customer mentality, and to value our distributors at the same time.

Challenges such as combining the best of Toro and Wheel Horse to provide benefits to all parties mean maintaining faith with everyone involved—something that requires both credibility and trust. Our historical practice was to plow under the values and unique characteristics of companies we had purchased by "Toroizing" them. But in this case, we chose to seed not sod because we wanted our people and those from Wheel Horse to recognize and integrate the strengths of each, and we wanted to make sure the value we were creating in combination exceeded what the entities offered by themselves. The Wheel Horse folks came to know that if they were willing to give Toro a chance, we would return that good faith by providing them every opportunity to succeed in their new environment.

The integration of Wheel Horse was consummated over a period of three years. A major conflict occurred when we moved the sales responsibility to our distributors, but overall the merger was a resounding success. Looking back, I would have stayed with some of the Wheel Horse ways longer, but that's hindsight. Both Toro and Wheel Horse continued to grow their businesses until the recession, and those distributors who aggressively accepted this new selling structure prospered. The fact that our Toro coworkers could speak openly and honestly of a supportive culture that worked for everyone went a long way toward backing up what the Wheel Horse newcomers might have otherwise considered "just talk." It reminded me, though, that new investments are absolutely vital and it pays to take the long view regarding their returns. Moreover, the way we make those investments pay us back is by demonstrating our adherence to mission and goals, and by "walking our talk" every day.

It was a different matter when we acquired Lawn-Boy, which had long been our most significant direct competitor. Now that Lawn-Boy is part of Toro, we'd like to sell as many Lawn-Boy products as we can, but it took us a long time to accept the idea that promoting and supporting Lawn-Boy were good things. We took the same approach as with Wheel Horse, and it really backfired. We had not done our "due diligence" well, and later uncovered major product quality and cost problems. Moreover, we purchased Lawn-Boy on the eve of the recession in the early nineties and that made a questionable acquisition look awful. But the real problem was that our distribution strategy was at odds with the Lawn-Boy management's mind-set.

We learned that managing from afar a team that was not dedicated to our marketing strategy was a death knell. We compromised the health and vitality not only of Lawn-Boy, but of our whole Consumer Division as well. Eventually, we got on track, did the things we needed to do, and while the seeds took longer to root and it took "weather conditions" longer than expected to turn favorable, we were able to preserve a sound strategy that eventually generated thick, green turf. Lawn-Boy is now positively embraced by the Toro organization and is exceeding our expectations in sales and profits.

This was a good illustration, as it turned out, of hanging in there to preserve the fundamental vision that drove the acquisition. Even our distributors, many of whom now carry both brands, see the long-view mission as wise and are supporting Lawn-Boy in ways no one could have imagined just a few years earlier.

Agents of Change

Time magazine featured "Planet Earth" as the cover story of the decade in January 1990. Extrapolating from current trends, the editors, predicting doom and gloom, said, "It doesn't look good, folks; in fact, the forecast calls for extinction." How then do we survive? How do we achieve green and clean? I may be in scarce company, but I believe in and even advocate personal responsibility.

Many people no longer believe they can be a source of change. I disagree. One of the greatest discoveries of our current generations is that human beings, by changing the inner attitudes of their minds, can change the outer aspects of their lives. We have the ability to deprogram ourselves from false or bad beliefs and move forward as agents of positive change. Your responsibility as a leader is to effect change, and you can do so by effecting real changes in your corporate climate and in your daily environment.

Work to involve your employees in goal-setting—involvement creates a sense of ownership with its many benefits. Provide effective positive reinforcement. As Ken Blanchard says in *The One-Minute Manager,* "Strive to catch people doing things right." Provide growth opportunities for your people: challenge them and help them build their confidence and develop their abilities. Build trust through openness and encourage honest two-way communication daily. This will permit you to foster risk taking, innovation, creativity, and the freedom to fail. Where there is freedom to fail, there is freedom to succeed.

Trust the process and recognize that processes take time. Can you recall the experience of neglecting your schoolwork only to be faced with a final exam you weren't ready for? An all-night study session was probably sufficient to pull off an acceptable grade despite a lack of advance preparation. Consider the results, however, if a farmer neglects the advance work required to plant and harvest a crop. No amount of last-ditch effort will produce the desired result because the process cannot be circumvented. Remember, you reap what you sow.

A Supportive Culture

The purpose of a corporate culture is to support your vision and enable your people to make the vision a reality. You'll find this is easiest in an environment that values everyone and encourages trust and open communications. Communicate without being judgmental. Analyze the action and its consequences rather than denigrate the person. When people seek your counsel or guidance, orient your comments toward the purpose—the action or outcome—rather than the person. Remember, too, that communication is more than talking, more than listening. When you've truly communicated, you've achieved mutual understanding, and mutual understanding implies actions and expectations. Make sure your follow-up is consistent with that understanding.

Find ways to encourage, recognize, and reinforce; give feedback, both positive and negative. At the same time, be sensitive to others' needs; take the time and be willing to care. Realize that people will behave more like owners if they know they can take responsibility and own up to error without fear. Be honest. Employees will know if your words or your actions are superficial or insincere. Accept that everyone has some inhibitions or reservations regarding change. Today, ongoing change is a way of doing business and may, for many, become a key "competitive edge." Keep this edge clean and sharp by helping your employees to see change as an opportunity for personal and professional growth and for increased job satisfaction.

World-class leaders today are people who are willing and able to translate cultural values into excellent performance. Translating cultural values into excellent performance requires leaders who can take risks, initiate, create, and innovate—and inspire their people to do the same. Leaders must learn to give power away; to serve and to channel that power to produce quality results that are reliable, responsive, and conform to requirements; and to put the customer first, last, and always. Move beyond your limits. Plant the seeds today that will enable you to become the excellent leader you can be.

The Harvest

IT WAS TIME for the harvest. The field crops were full and abundant. The lawn was green and lush; it was reaching full growth but was still in process, still becoming. As Lee Durr thought back over his work—preparing the soil, seeding, cultivating, and nurturing—a pervasive sense of gratification overcame him, not only from the bountiful reward in the field and lawn but also from the personal growth and development of the men and women who had worked with him, who had been a part of the husbandry. And of course, Lee himself had grown.

It was all part of the harvest. Much of it Lee expected. But the surprise was that various fruits of the harvest cropped up not just at the end, but *during the cycle* and in unexpected ways. The surprises continued throughout the season. Lee understood that this was a part of the natural law of the harvest and would be repeated over and over. The harvest was rich indeed.

Results are important: in fact, results are essential both in the short term and in the long run. Getting results is a key leadership requirement; a company must be financially viable to sustain itself. But not all results are financial. Several nonfinancial results directly affect profitability. Other results, worthy in their own right, may generate a propensity for profits and returns. Still other results transcend economics. These are important too; in fact, the longer the leader leads, the more important they become. These final results that go beyond the company's financial record may be the ultimate harvest that comes from stewardship, the leader attribute that insures the future. And it may be these results that, as Stephen Covey provokes us to think about in *The Seven Habits of Highly Effective People,* will be our epitaph.

CHAPTER THIRTEEN

Real Bottom-Line Results

"What is Real?" asked the Rabbit one day. "Does it mean having things that buzz inside you and a stick-out handle?"

"Real isn't how you are made," said the Skin Horse. "It's a thing that happens to you. When a child loves you for a long, long time, not just to play with, but really loves you, then you become Real."

"Does it hurt?"

"Sometimes." For he was always truthful. "When you are Real you don't mind being hurt."

"Does it happen all at once, like being wound up, or bit by bit?"

"It doesn't happen all at once. You become. It takes a long time. That's why it doesn't often happen to people who break easily, or who have sharp edges, or who have to be carefully kept. Generally, by the time you are Real, most of your hair has been loved off, and your eyes drop out, and you get loose in the joints and very shabby. But these things don't matter at all, because once you are Real you can't be ugly, except to people who don't understand."

— MARGERY WILLIAMS,
THE VELVETEEN RABBIT

HOW DO REAL RESULTS come about? The harvest we all hope for in the fall, or at the end of the fiscal year, will come about naturally if we follow the time-honored laws of the harvest. After the farmer prepares the soil, plants his seeds, and then carefully nurtures the emerging plants, he waits anxiously for the time he can harvest a crop. We, too, look forward to the outcome or result of our plans and efforts. When we follow natural laws and principles, we reap real results over time. Time becomes our friend and ally, not our enemy. The laws of nature, the laws that govern the harvest, are on our side.

Often the results we get come slowly as a welcomed consequence of observing natural laws. They rise from deep-rooted values. The harvest of those values in an organization may be likened to the growth of a bamboo tree. When the bamboo tree is planted, nothing happens for four years, except possibly a small sprout. Imagine: for a very long period nothing happens above the surface where it can be seen and measured! But underground the roots are being nurtured and strengthened. Then in the fifth year, the bamboo tree grows some eighty feet! It takes a long time, but patience is rewarded with great growth.

A value-based culture, a bone-deep commitment to quality, a comprehensive focus on the customer, and real innovation—these things take time to grow. Core values take a long time to root and sprout. It takes a very patient, focused, and disciplined management team to keep the organization moving toward its mission and holding to its long-term strategies so that the fruits of the harvest can be realized. Along the way, we can expect all sorts of upsets, uncertainties, and surprises.

Harvest along the Way

We often have such a preoccupation with "the bottom line" that we ignore or compromise the processes needed to harvest the fruits of our work. If the bottom line is financial success, it comes about best when each individual does his or her job as well as possible. If the bottom line is a team goal or a broad organizational goal, it too is best met by specific individual efforts. Collective, corporate outcomes are realized as individuals contribute positive attitudes and behaviors in the processes that lead to success. As we continuously improve our product and service quality, the natural consequence over time is increased shareholder return on investment through strong financial performance.

In Toro's fiscal year 1993, it was an important goal to make one dollar earnings-per-share. But it was really the learning process, the discipline, and the seeds we planted that gave Toro not only an impressive financial result but also great momentum and confidence to accelerate through the end of the fiscal year and into the future. These positive results no doubt would have occurred if our earnings-per-share had been ninety-nine cents or even ninety cents. Still, meeting the goal was important to our people.

In our monthly huddles, we reviewed the "great plays" of the past month. I talked a lot about us as a winning team and tried to build team spirit among the employees. From the time of our recovery from the 1992 recession, these meetings helped build a sense of worth, value, and team among the employees. I worried, though, that with all the emphasis on turning around the company—as measured by the goal of one dollar earnings-per-share—the employees would not have that winning team feeling if our profits fell short.

When we turned in a loss for fiscal year 1992, with some horrendous restructuring charges, our local paper ranked us the "number one loser" in the Minneapolis area. I kept the article posted to my office wall until the final huddle of 1993. I didn't want our team to feel like losers if we fell short of the goal of one dollar earnings-per-share. So I asked our employees at the huddle to raise their hands if they worked at Toro the year before, when we were "losers" in the newspaper's view. About 97 percent of the people raised their hands, making my point that this was a winning team even if the company lost money in 1992 or didn't make the fiscal 1993 goal. What made us a great team was the individual sacrifices, the spirit, the great plays, and the momentum from the employees as they turned the company's financial situation around. I burned the article ceremoniously in front of the employees—to their cheers and delight.

The fact that we achieved $1.05 earnings-per-share in fiscal 1993 was important to us. It illustrated the importance of focus, team work, goal setting, and sacrifice. But it didn't make us a great team. We harvested the goodness of Toro all through the year. In the total scheme of things, the one dollar earnings-per-share wasn't the essential thing. What was essential was what we accomplished during the journey. We see this truth more clearly as time and distance separate us from the events.

When we have a macro-perspective of time and events, we see more clearly that purpose and vision and progress may be as important as meeting short-term goals. In fact, if your goals are too short term, meeting them may inhibit you from building the organization and maintaining the health of the company properly. While one-year goals are important, I suggest that you focus on five-year goals. This focus frees you to harvest more value along the way, and to devote more time, more dollars, and more resources to the processes without the end or the goal pressuring you for suboptimal quick fixes.

Short-term goals can often move you off the real purpose, especially as you get closer to them. You often begin to behave unnaturally, working against the laws of nature just to meet a goal that often turns out to be superficial or superfluous. Goals provide a direction, a way to measure progress, a way to keep on track. But remember that there are natural cycles and principles beyond the goal that operate irrespective of its achievement.

The Learning Organization

W. Edwards Deming, the revered pioneer of the quality movement, made a point that goes to the heart of the issues and challenges facing us as leaders. He said, "Our prevailing system of management has destroyed our people. People are born with intrinsic motivation, self-respect, joy in learning. The destruction starts with toddlers. A prize for the best Halloween costume, gold stars, grades in schools, and on up through the universities. On the job, people, teams, divisions are ranked—reward for the one at the top—punishment for the one at the bottom; management by objectives, incentives paid, business plans, put together separately cause further loss, unknown and unknowable." As Deming expressed it, "There's only one basic problem: our institutions are inconsistent with human nature. Human beings are designed to learn; learning is one of our most basic impulses."

I heard Peter M. Senge, author of *The Fifth Discipline: The Art and Practice of the Learning Organization,* speak at a leadership forum a couple of years ago about how organizations can truly *learn* and continually enhance their ability to achieve their goals. He noted that all five disciplines—personal mastery, mental models, team learning, shared vision, and systems thinking—must be operating simultaneously in your organization for this to really occur. What caught my attention was the way he described two of the five discipline components: shared vision and systems thinking. Senge charges, "Today a lot of people talk about vision and they mainly talk about shared visions in our organizations. It's hard to find a CEO today who doesn't want to learn how to build better shared visions. But very few people are recognizing the extent to which shared visions are really nothing if they're not rooted in people's personal visions."

The systems thinking component challenges us to continually look for renewing processes that provide structure for taking effective action. According to Senge, "In learning organizations, learning is a process of enhancing knowledge, and that knowledge gives us the capacity for effective action." Senge characterized learning organizations as ones that continuously ask two questions: "(1) What are we trying to create? and (2) What are we learning about how to do it? Learning is about the enhancement of capacity; learning is about being able to do something—to produce something, to create something, to achieve something—that you couldn't before."

As we search for ways to insure our competitive advantage, we must look beyond traditional thinking. Senge teaches us that "the word *learn* in Chinese is constructed from two symbols. One means *study* or *take in* and the other means *practice* constantly. You cannot think or express the word *learn* without thinking or expressing ongoing study and practice. The root source of competitive advantage is not technology, not a market niche, not even a reputation or brand name. The root source of competitive advantage is an organization's relative ability to learn and share together. All other things are fleeting. Technologies can be copied. Market reputations come and go." The competitive advantage resides in creative capability—to continuously create new technologies, new marketing and distribution possibilities, innovative new products, or new value-added services. And you do this by continuously learning.

Genuine involvement by people who are empowered to do what they do best in an environment of trust is the key to value-added contributions. This empowerment nurtures the individual's sense of worth, and when self-worth grows, people grow. They will then take on more responsibility, contribute more, and become more purposeful in their role in the organization. This positive feedback loop illustrates characteristics of a cyclical, natural law, similar to the natural laws that govern growing grass.

If in their attempt to scale the fifteen-hundred-foot face of El Capitan in Yosemite National Park, tandem rock climbers are confronted with a route that they've never experienced before, they need to learn as they go. Tandem rock climbers behave as you hope a two-person learning organization might. They begin the climb with a shared vision. One climber develops a path up a rock face while the other belays him on the ground, protecting him from falling by securing him with the other end of the rope. The lead climber is learning the best route and teaching the belayer his route at the same time. Once the lead climber has managed a distance near the end of his rope, about 165 feet, he anchors himself with his end of the rope in order to belay the second climber. This climber can then follow the path of the first, and even climb up another 150 feet or so. In this way they exchange roles all the way up the mountain.

If these climbers don't operate *inter*dependently, neither will make it. Both climbers must learn all the way up the mountain. In that learning process, they experience a bonding of the spirit. They become a self-taught team, stronger in the realization that they are interdependent. Quality and excellence grow as team members recognize their interdependency. When this happens on the job, an organization becomes a learning organization. In an environment of trust, team members learn and teach at the same time because they are interdependent.

In rock climbing the route is often obscure, demanding that the team be flexible and transform itself when necessary to make its way through the challenges. When an organization develops flexibility, it can renew itself through learning and recycling. Each cycle begins on a new plateau and different outcomes occur. Toro is an example of this continuous learning process: it recycles again and again because of the forces of continuous improvement, market changes, new technologies, competitive initiatives, etc. (Fitting, I suppose, since we make the Recycler lawn mower.) Ed Land, founder of Polaroid, used to have a plaque on his wall that said, "A mistake is an event—the full benefit of which has not yet been turned to your advantage." Now that is a characteristic of a learner!

Is Winning Everything?

I'm reminded of Gary Smith's story in *Sports Illustrated* about coach Jim Valvano. Suffering from terminal spinal cancer at the age of forty-seven, Valvano, the former North Carolina State basketball coach, looked back on his life and told a story about himself as a twenty-three-year-old coach of a small college team. "Why is winning so important to you?" the players asked Valvano. "Because the final score defines you," he said. "You lose, and you're a loser. You win, and you're a winner." "No," the players insisted, "participation is what matters. Trying your best, regardless of whether you win or lose—that's what defines you."

It took Valvano twenty-four more years of living. It took the coach bolting up from the mattress three or four times a night with his T-shirt soaked with sweat and his teeth rattling from the chill of chemotherapy and the terror of seeing himself die repeatedly in his dreams. It took all that for him to say it: "Those kids were right. It's effort, not result. It's trying. God, what a great human being I could have been if I'd had this awareness back then."

Valvano learned that winning isn't everything, but winning *is* important. And the leader's job is to create the environment that motivates people to winning performances. As Meg Wheatley points out in *Leadership and the New Science,* leaders don't really motivate people at the roots; ultimately, people are motivated from within. If you believe that your employees have great potential and that they desire to contribute and be of value, then you've laid the foundation for their own motivation. People tend to be self-motivated *if they're valued.* So the leader's mission is to create an environment for personal as well as corporate growth. If employees operate in an environment that values them and their contributions, they will work toward the common good—and the organization will invariably thrive.

The importance of the work environment to the individual surfaces on many levels. Obviously, the work environment is important to the person's livelihood, but the best environments also enrich the individual's life and free the individual to contribute more to the goals of the company. The best environments also give the individual a chance to learn the importance of interdependency, a value rarely learned in the institutions of our competitive society. As thoughtful human beings, we should not be surprised by the interdependence between ourselves and others at every stage of our lives, from cradle to grave. In our work environments, we are interdependent in skills, knowledge, and resources. We are more fulfilled when our endeavors touch others and give meaning to their lives and their work.

At Toro our corporate environment, like many others, is open and increasingly pluralistic, characterized by the collision of values and agendas of people who are trying to forge the corporate vision and mission, while at the same time trying to sustain the many individual and subcultural identities in the organization. A corporate culture is wrought out of the company's values and behaviors. But within that culture, many subcultures emerge.

Every organization faces the inevitable tension between personal freedom and the need for all employees to be governed by core values and principles. The challenge is to find a way to honor and preserve the freedom that allows us to be the best people we can be, while understanding that personal liberation is meaningful only if it serves a culture and value structure, and only if it helps move the company toward its vision. For example, Irv Hockaday, CEO of Hallmark Cards, recognizes the many subcultures within his very diverse employee group. At the same time, he works hard to drive home the core values of Hallmark. Thus, diverse cultures can exist within a larger framework because all employees operate on the same basic principles.

Similarly, management and employees alike must balance increasingly contradictory pressures between short-term financial performance and long-term growth initiatives. As processes in our corporate environments are emphasized more, employees often interpret this as a substitute for bottom-line focus. But we need both, not one or the other. Performance issues must be integrated properly with people issues. A focus on the people side will lead to employees' personal fulfillment and improved company performance, but at the same time, austerity spending practices, right sizing, and tenacious operating excellence are necessary conditions for competing globally.

Corporations face an increasing need for investment in processes, equipment, systems, new products, and human development. There's an increasing requirement to apply new technologies and innovation, even with all the attendant risks. Paradoxically, these risks are often mitigated by the quest for zero defects, for "doing it right the first time," and for reliability and consistency. One new reality of the marketplace is that all of these contradictory pressures must be dealt with and optimized together. Toro is a good example of a company in a quest to integrate old values and new thinking. With all our imperfections, we exhibit the strong combination of innovation and reliability, merging individual freedom with group collaboration.

"Living" the Culture

Recently a group of us at Toro felt that our culture might need a shot in the arm. People weren't talking about PIE much, and we weren't seeing a lot of the culture activities we had seen previously. One member of our group made an important observation, however. She felt that the Pride In Excellence culture had become ingrained in our people. Our value system had been practiced long enough and by enough of us that it had become integrated into our beings. It seemed to her that the reason employees were not overtly "doing" culture things in the name of Pride In Excellence was because they were "living" the cultural values every day—automatically, silently, with no fanfare—because the values had become a part of who they were. *Eureka!* What a fruit of the harvest! We were beginning to transform ourselves to a new level of behavior. We were now moving to true interdependency.

This transformation leads to new levels of success. Richard Pascale, author of the popular *Zen and the Art of Management,* suggests the reason why the Japanese have outperformed Americans in so many industries is not only because they know how to effectively change what they do, but also because they actually change who they are, their very being. The Japanese call this continuous altering of one's inner being *kokoro.* The reason why many organizational transformation initiatives don't work on a sustained basis—despite all the techniques, technology, and management tools available—is that people (especially leaders) fail to transform their own being, their attitudes and nature. The Japanese believe that just doing things better and better is meaningless unless the people become wiser and deeper in the process.

Take quality as an example: if you want high quality products, you can't afford to have anyone in the production process merely conforming to the quality methods. Real quality only comes when people have an inner drive to do their best. All the guidelines, procedures, techniques, tools, and training in the world won't insure excellent quality. The leader needs to cultivate an environment that nurtures peoples' accountability, pride, and involvement. The leadership practice of serving, of supporting and coaching the organization, enables the team to reach new heights in quality by encouraging the transformation of each individual's inner being.

For that transformation to begin, however, leaders have to transform themselves. As Janet Hagberg describes in *Real Power,* servant leaders actually become more powerful as they move power and contribution down through the organization. Their inner being becomes wiser, more insightful, and authentic as they let go of the symbolic levels of power and control, and focus on helping their employees increase their own power and contribution. This is happening now at Toro, and every day we see gratifying examples of true personal growth in individuals.

Sometimes the outside world sees those examples, too. Earlier I introduced you to Jim Seifert, assistant general counsel for Toro. He shared his story of how he and his team found new ways to reduce the company's risks and costs due to product liability (see page 44). As a result of that team's creativity and willingness to find a new way to tackle an old problem, Toro received the Significant Achievement Award in the Application of Alternative Dispute Resolutions presented by The Center for Public Resources Institute for Dispute Resolutions. I want to share some of Jim's acceptance speech:

> FIVE YEARS AGO at The Toro Company we started with a blank sheet of paper and asked a simple question: "How can we take control of our product liability risk?" Clearly, waiting for a lawsuit to be filed, responding with standard discovery, engaging in expensive motions, taking depositions, and hoping a jury would see the world our way was positively the worst approach to achieving the goal.
>
> If there is any secret to what we have done, it is that five years ago we defined our product liability problem first and foremost as a human problem, and secondly—a very distant second—as a legal problem. Viewing a claim or lawsuit as a human problem opened up our minds to a completely new set of tools and strategies for solving very complex issues.

Instead of stating to the injured person, through our lawyers, "You're wrong and we're right," we now sit in the living rooms of our customers and listen. We empathize with the reality of a life that will never be the same. We admit when we're wrong and we explain in simple language when we're right. If we can't agree, we find a reliable third party to structure a fact-based discussion that usually leads to resolution.

At the end of the day, we have closure of a risk, a customer for life, and at the same time, we have left the claimant with his or her individual dignity intact.

Thank you very much for this award. We will cherish it.

These words from a Toro employee make me proud to be a servant leader. These words bring the realization that our culture has become an integral part of who we are as a company and as individuals. The fruits of the harvest are sweet indeed.

We continue to build our Pride In Excellence culture to transcend our own individual orientations but still give voice and value to our separate identities and traditions. It's an audacious, complex, risky, and daunting task. Part of the harvest is witnessing how the organization and management balance and optimize these apparent paradoxes, how they work through and adapt to the constant tension, bringing the company and its constituency to new heights of growth and well-being. Some may fear, given the trends, that the harvest will become increasingly difficult as our business and social worlds become more complex and stressful. But I have a calm reassurance that good fruits come from good soil, seed, and care. As we preserve and beautify our own turf, we observe the law of the harvest.

In business, the fruits of the harvest come naturally as *by-products* of properly building an organization and environment for personal and corporate growth. They are not characteristically the object of our work. As we pursue our goals, putting into practice the understanding that soil preparation plus seed plus sound turf management equals harvest, an organization emerges that can:

- continuously grow and sustain competitiveness and leadership;

- overcome, resist, and get through crises like weather problems and recessions;

- operate as a team and embrace new ideas and initiatives collectively;

- maintain an environment where learning enhances knowledge, and that knowledge increases capacity for effective action; and

- achieve the long-term goals of the corporation.

The fruits of the harvest include the creation of an organization where management continuously asks "What are we trying to create?" and "What are we learning about how to do it?"; an organization where management builds trust by freeing employees to learn, even during times of recession and recovery, stress and chaos; an organization where people operate as a team, sacrificing individual objectives and initiating innovative change to improve products, systems, and processes to better meet customer needs; an organization where employees operate like owners, assuming responsibility and accountability, where managers are coaches and leaders are servants, and where people are focused on core competencies and fundamental strengths as well as new business opportunities and innovations; and finally an organization where people have high aspirations and stretch to reach new levels of performance while embracing core values, beliefs, and governing principles.

CHAPTER FOURTEEN

The Grass Can Be Greener on Your Side

One thing I know, the only ones among you who will be really happy are those who will have sought and found how to serve.
— ALBERT SCHWEITZER

WE COMMONLY THINK that the grass is greener on the other side of the fence. In reality, it often is not, nor does it have to be. Every job or role is fraught with problems and challenges. Life is not an easy road, and from a larger perspective, this is fortunate. The good news is that turning problems into solutions and opportunities, or even learning to cope, makes a person wiser, healthier, and more productive. Overcoming opposition gives people more confidence and security, moves them toward their potential, and gives them a greater sense of achievement, purpose, and worth.

Forbes magazine devoted its entire September 1992 issue to the question, "If things are so good in America, why do we feel so bad?" Several of America's best writers and scholars, including John Updike and Saul Bellow, addressed this question. Many of the writers indicated that one reason for our discontent is a loss of trust in our institutions, systems, and ideas. Peggy Noonan, author of *What I Saw at the Revolution* and *Liberty and the Pursuit of Happiness,* put forward another reason why we feel so bad that particularly appealed to me. She wrote that Americans today expect to find ultimate happiness here and now; in fact, many feel entitled to it. She noted that people used to be more accepting of unhappiness and that the search for the good life has now become more of a search for the "life of goods." If our quest for the life of goods replaces a higher form of stewardship, the age of entitlement will negate our sense of purpose and meaning, making it difficult to see the lush green grass that we stand on.

We can make our grass greener if we want to by working with the laws of nature, living in harmony with nature, and cultivating our turf with the tools we have. The grass on the other side of the fence is not our stewardship. If life is indeed a mystery, as Noonan reminds us, then Voltaire is right that we must cultivate our own garden to make it as green as nature will allow.

The feeling of entitlement seems contrary to the attitude of previous generations. Our ancestors were much more inclined to a life of contentment as opposed to a pursuit of happiness. Contentment connotes a sense of long-term harmony with life. Although there are short-term ups and downs, life in general is okay and we can accept the strife of life as a balance against the good things that come along. A close friend of mine once sent me a greeting card, and on the cover it read, "Happiness is an inside job." Inside the card it said, "Listen to the wisdom of your heart." We aren't going to find happiness or contentment outside of ourselves. It will only happen within ourselves. But happiness today has become a short-term fix or band-aid remedy because we link our happiness to recognition and possessions—a new job, a raise, a new home or car—or to having things happen in our lives. But such happiness dissipates quickly. Unless good things happen frequently, we become unhappy. With the focus on the hype that so often accompanies our daily life, we seem to need those quick fixes more and more to sustain a sense of happiness as opposed to a long-term feeling of contentment.

Weathering Crises

Since I've been the CEO at Toro, we've experienced two recessionary crises. The first almost wrecked the company and the second could have been equally catastrophic. Crises do funny things to people. They jolt us out of our comfort zones—out of the security of normalcy and certainty—disrupting our routines and adding a great deal of stress and discontinuity. On the other hand, crises and chaos can create positive change for a couple of reasons. First, people invariably reprioritize their time and energies to focus on the things that are most important to them and give up the things that aren't. Second, because the crisis is so overwhelming, people let go of their normal paradigms and their traditional boundaries, realizing they don't work anymore.

In times of chaos, having meaningful core values and an overarching purpose can galvanize an organization. If employees identify with the values, believe in them, and trust that the leadership stands firm behind them, the organization remains vital, even when the structure changes and the processes are reengineered. People can still make sense of things. New patterns may emerge, but they will still be centered on principles that reflect the organization's identity and purpose. Having core beliefs in place, you can move through the crisis more effectively because you can trust that people will rally around those beliefs. In companies with strong core values, clear identity, and noble purpose, employees tend to center their own behavior around principles and beliefs rather than policies or procedures, which are easily changeable.

Chaos often signals the beginning of a new order as a whole new set of interrelationships and boundaries emerge. Chaos becomes a powerful catalyst for rethinking and reengineering the company. Advocates of chaos theory suggest that the primary benefit of chaos is that it eventually brings the organization to a new life, often with breakthrough ideas and form. Organizations don't need to die if they can survive chaos by reorganizing themselves to fit the new environment. While we are often terrified of chaos, it is a natural state. True change comes best and easiest when things are out of equilibrium. Since the alternative is to die, we eventually take the risk to adapt to a new environment.

No Turning Back

I've heard Toro people say, "I wish we could go back to the way we used to be." Or "We were such a close family company way back when." As we emerge from crisis, there is always the hope that things will return to "normal" or "as they once were." But they never do, and this is actually a blessing. A business would have trouble competing if it returned to the alleged "good old days." I've often said, particularly after a recession, that "business as usual" is illusionary. The past is always the past and it can't be re-created.

For me, the point of *Jurassic Park* is that we can't re-create the past. We can't go back to a previous age or time. Why would we want to go back to the past anyway? While we might make some things operate as before, we can't make everything the same because we are interdependent with the environment, which has also changed from the crisis. It's folly to think that just because the past was plentiful with goodness and we learned how to operate successfully in it, it was better. The future will be different; but if we are proactive and have a progressive and positive attitude, we can fashion the future to work for us; we can learn to make change our ally.

As we go from crisis to crisis, we observe this law of nature: *things have a way of repeating themselves.* In most cycles, this is illusionary since things are usually not quite the same after a chaotic period. Green grass sprouts each spring, but because winter disturbs the soil differently each year, it is not actually the same grass as before. Businesses are like that too. They don't come through economic cycles or selling seasons to return to how they were. Organizations must continually adapt to become fluid. The "seamless" organization is always searching and stretching beyond the old boundaries.

The farmer is familiar with the cycle of nature. He prepares the soil; he seeds; he patiently manages the crop; then he reaps what he has sown. This cycle repeats itself over and over, although each season he tries to get better, using newer tools, better seeds, and different fertilizers. But each year, his work is subject to the changing conditions of nature. The yields vary, often improving with the next cycle, yet sometimes they do not.

New cycles bring a blend of sameness and difference, a blend of traditions and new ideas and responses. The danger in coming through the turbulent part of the cycle is the desire to return to the basics, to seek the comfort of old traditions, instead of adapting traditions and bringing them forward into the future. The challenge is to blend the values of the past with the new realities of the future. As the organization adapts and reshapes itself, the harvest changes. Organizations go through continuous cycles of recession, recovery, new initiatives, growth, and new plateaus.

Time and cycles can alter aspects of some goals or priorities, but fundamental goals and values invariably endure. Principles and core values, like good seed and soil, are important to have as a foundation whenever we have to move through crisis or chaos—conditions that are becoming more normal all the time. When leaders have grounded the organization in core values, principles, and purpose that people can trust, the new behavior patterns that emerge from the cycle will reflect this foundation. Thus, the mission and vision of the company will stay intact.

One at a Time

Author M. Scott Peck begins *The Road Less Traveled* with the rather stark assertion, "Life is difficult." Any student of agriculture knows that the harvest is often in doubt in spite of the good planning and hard work of the growers. The weather can be harsh, surprising, punishing. And other factors in the environment—including social, economic, and political trends—can impact the harvest.

Given this uncertainty, many growers (and leaders) seek to control as much as they can. They hope for a measure of predictability.

But in their efforts to insure an adequate return on investment for all who have a stake in the venture, leaders often try to impose initiatives, programs, and ideas that have succeeded elsewhere. In their attempts to clone companies and guarantee success, leaders invariably fail because each organization has its own culture, paradigms, processes, and systems.

We need to see that things could be better (the grass could be greener) on our side of the fence, if we decide to make it so—if we want to grow our own turf, create a healthy environment, and nurture it. Each individual has to decide that he or she can make a difference. And it often comes down to the little things, like helping an employee start his car with your jumper cables in the bitter cold when everyone else has gone home. Or after a big corporate event is over, sticking around to help clean up the mess. Such "little things" reinforce the servant leadership model and make the leader a more human and real mentor.

Once, after a Toro Employee Day function, several employees—including some of the officers who made presentations—stayed around to help with cleanup. They folded the chairs, stacked them, and some picked up the garbage. Observing this was a man whom Toro had hired to help put on the audiovisual show. He had listened to the speeches—to, as he termed it, "the pontification and folderol" about leadership and culture—with much cynicism. But when he saw the managers working side-by-side with the other employees to do the "dirty work," he came over to me and said, "Your management team just told me more about leadership and quality than all the speeches and presentations put together. Seeing you all here to the very end, cleaning up with the other employees, is great. That's my kind of leadership!" In the end, a "little thing" like helping to clean up communicates more than anything what servant leadership is all about.

Participating in events such as Employee Day not only enriches our lives and enlarges our capacity to work together, but it also gives us energy to serve, help, and teach others. Sometimes it takes an outsider to see the magic of the moment, to see the beauty of the fruit of the harvest, to shed new light on the experience, or to note the impact of the group or team. Sometimes when we can see things from a new perspective, we can become enlightened to a new reality of our experiences.

Harold Shapiro, president of Princeton University, reminded us in his address to the graduating class of 1993 that in Greek mythology, a god or goddess often bestowed a capacity beyond human knowing on an individual mortal being, if only for a brief moment. The mortal was able for that short period to see reality in a much more objective and comprehensive way. It would often help if, in our world, we could catch a glimpse of ourselves and our situation as they really are, without the distortion that our own personal history and prejudices create, which limits our understanding. If we had a window through which we could see, at least fleetingly, the full possibilities of ourselves and our organizations, we might pursue our work more vigorously. From this shared illumination, we might draw the strength, energy, and enthusiasm to move forward and build our future.

We all want the grass to be greener and we can make the grass greener on our side. It's a matter of attitude and action. My attitude, my conscious decision, is that my side of the fence is, or at least can be, greener than the other side. If you assume accountability for your own turf and operate with the attitude that you can make a difference, you'll work proactively to make your environment the best that it possibly can be. If, on the other hand, you are preoccupied with your own scarcities and deficiencies—as opposed to recognizing the great abundance that you have—you will be looking to other, seemingly greener, pastures for solutions and happiness.

Often there are small but magical moments that illustrate not only to outsiders but to ourselves and our associates that our goals and dreams can be achieved by working together for a common good, even if it means personal sacrifice. It can be hard to persuade some individuals that they ought to make a personal sacrifice or even that they can make a difference in an organization. The "can't do" attitude is often the reason for lazy people and stagnant organizations. I want people at Toro to believe that they can make a difference because they do make a difference. Leaders are incapable of moving mountains without followers.

Peter Block, author of *Stewardship,* exhorts leaders to focus on stewardship of physical and human assets and to allow and encourage individuals to incorporate the call to action into their daily lives. We can only solve our business and environmental problems by solving them ourselves. The solution is often within our domain without our realizing it. But we need to have the willingness, the courage, and the conviction to take individual action.

The Rainbow Connection

The metaphor of the "pot of gold at the end of the rainbow" is a strange one. It's as if there's no real goal to reach because everyone knows that the end of the rainbow is just an illusion. In the song "The Rainbow Connection" from *The Muppet Movie* (the story of Kermit the Frog and his journey to Hollywood to make a movie), Kermit sings: "Rainbows are visions, but only illusions, and rainbows have nothing to hide." Why undertake a journey in vain? Kermit continues: "So we've been told, and some choose to believe it. I know they're wrong; wait and see."

In the movie, Kermit demonstrates that the pot of gold is not at the journey's end. Instead, nuggets of gold are found during the journey, all along the way. The harvest occurs during the cycle and repeats itself. It is a never-ending process. The harvest isn't necessarily reaching a particular point in time or a specific goal. When I watched *The Muppet Movie* with my youngest daughter, I thought I was watching a children's movie. But something drove me to watch it again as an adult. That's when I realized that there was a significant adult message—that the harvest occurs during the journey, within the cycle.

In March 1987, I took a management team on a three-day retreat to talk about our corporate culture and the philosophy that drives my personal vision and mission. It was a time for me to share my core values, beliefs, and sense of purpose. It was a time for me,

Ken Melrose, to speak from the heart, not a time for the chief executive to speak only from the head. I felt that the team needed to understand what my purpose and core values were all about, and I felt strongly that these had to be at the root of our culture.

During the retreat, I showed the group two movies. The first was Jim Henson's *The Muppet Movie*. The idea behind *The Muppet Movie* is to follow your dream, to pursue your goals at the end of the rainbow. In the movie, Kermit the Frog decides to leave his home in the Okefenokee swamp to pursue his dream of making a movie in Hollywood. Throughout his travels he has to overcome many obstacles—the main one being the villain, Doc Hopper, who wants Kermit to be the spokesperson for a frog legs fast-food restaurant. Doc Hopper repeatedly tries to stop Kermit from pursuing his own goal of reaching Hollywood and making a movie.

Undaunted, Kermit extricates himself from all the traps set by the villain. Along the way, he begins to collect members of the Muppet company—Miss Piggy, Fozzy Bear, Gonzo, and others— and the growing entourage joins him in his quest. Near the end of the movie, Kermit and company reach the Painted Desert in Arizona. Kermit walks away from the group for a moment, and as he gazes at the stars wonders what he is doing. He begins to question the purpose of his journey and doubts that he'll achieve his goal of making the movie. A sense of failure begins to creep into the movie.

One of the Muppets comes up to him to find out why he seems so pensive and sad. Kermit explains his feeling of failure, and the Muppet says, "No, you've already succeeded. Look what's happened to all these Muppets. You've brought great happiness and purpose to their lives, and it happened along the way during the journey to Hollywood," along the journey to the rainbow's end.

Finally in Hollywood, Kermit begins his movie only to have it fail because Gonzo breaks the props. Everything crashes, whereupon the movie ends and the audience is left pondering the question: Did Kermit achieve his goal or didn't he? The answer, of course, is yes, but certainly not in the sense that we were led to expect in the beginning.

According to "The Rainbow Connection," there is no such thing as the end of the rainbow, no pot of gold. But Kermit does suggest there's more to it than that. He learns that the important stuff happens during the journey. And so he learns what "The Rainbow Connection" is. *The Muppet Movie* is a children's way of telling us adults that the harvest occurs along the road as we're moving toward our dreams and visions—and that we, as leaders, need to be mindful of what's happening around us as we lead, coach, and serve, as we relate with other people who are influenced by our quest and our ideas.

The Wise Man or Woman

The second movie we viewed on the retreat was *The Fourth Wise Man* starring Martin Sheen. The movie was adapted from the book *The Story of the Other Wise Man* by Henry Van Dyke. I hoped that this film would also help enlighten my management team to the reality that the harvest occurs during the journey and that it's a never-ending process—we will never reach the goal of having an ideal culture; we will never reach a final plateau by a certain point in time.

The Fourth Wise Man is a story about Artaban, another wise man who was called, just as the other three wise men were, by the Star of David. He lives in a neighboring land, but he is told that he can catch up with the other three wise men if he hurries to meet them in Jerusalem as they congregate there before continuing on to Bethlehem. Like the others, Artaban brings three gifts of kingly value—a sapphire, a ruby, and a pearl.

Before he gets to Jerusalem, he helps a man alongside the road who has been robbed and beaten and is dying. Artaban is able to restore that person's health, but he has to use one of his jewels. It also detains him such that he's too late to meet the other wise men. So he hurries on his own to Bethlehem, but Jesus, Joseph, and Mary have fled to Egypt. He then begins his trek to Egypt, and along the way he comes across a leper colony in desperate need of a "medicine man" to serve them. He ends up spending thirty-three years in the leper colony, expending another jewel to help the lepers. He can't seem to leave because they continue to depend on him, so he stays to serve them.

When news is received that Jesus has returned to Jerusalem, Artaban decides to leave the colony. When he arrives in Jerusalem, the daughter of one of his old friends from his homeland has been captured by Roman soldiers, and he gives up his third gift in order to free her. As in the past, that act detains him and he misses Jesus carrying the cross through the jeering crowds toward Mt. Calvary. As fate would have it, Artaban has a heart attack as he struggles to catch up to Jesus. He recovers somewhat, but not enough to go forward, and he slumps to the ground.

In the end, after the crucifixion, Jesus appears to Artaban as he is dying. Artaban reaches for his bag and, realizing he has no more gifts, he turns to Jesus to say he has failed Him, that he has given away his gifts and has nothing to give Him, unlike the other three wise men. Artaban feels like a failure who has let down his King. Whereupon Jesus speaks that famous line, "Whatsoever you do unto my brother, you do unto me," meaning of course he has already served Jesus by ministering to God's people all during his life. Thus he has not failed Jesus after all. The harvest for Artaban came along the way, during the journey, and not at the end.

These two stories illustrate that the process can be more significant than the destination. We're all on a journey. We're all going somewhere. Some of us know our destinations, others do not. Both Kermit and Artaban knew their destination but discounted their journey as only a means to it. "The Rainbow Connection" is the path between the end and where we are today. The significance of the vision or the dream, as Kermit learned, was going for it, not necessarily getting there.

In a competitive environment, the focus is on end results; that is both appropriate and necessary. But the final score, the year-end earnings-per-share, the number of units sold, the number of defects, the closing price of the stock can often distract us. If we could see the enterprise in terms of continuums, cycles, and ongoing processes for change and growth, we could recognize and pluck additional fruits to be harvested. In these two films, both Kermit the Frog and Artaban experience the harvest without even recognizing it. Through their vision and perseverance, however, they were able to transform not only their lives but the lives of others.

The Winner at the Finish Line

In the final analysis, the question remains: "What is the compelling reason for leading from your principles, for practicing servant leadership, for managing by genuinely valuing others?" And you may further ask, "Are you assured more growth over the long run? Are you guaranteed more profit?" The answer, unfortunately, is "maybe, and maybe not." Autocratic, top-down, efficiency-driven, and devaluing leadership styles may yield better financial results over the short term. Turnover will likely be higher, but that may refresh the organization and encourage change and new ideas. If the only objective of the leader is to satisfy the shareholders or owners, many systems and styles can work to achieve this goal for a period of time. I know from my own experience, however, that principle-centeredness, valuing people, and servant leadership together can also satisfy the financial requirements of the owners.

Beyond meeting financial requirements, servant leadership creates greener grass on your side, and it creates stronger "reserves" to endure periods of stress due to economic pressures, competitive warfare, or other factors, such as unfavorable weather conditions. While not always efficient, servant leadership creates a very effective and supportive environment. You can then call upon this stored asset to marshall heroic efforts and sacrifices for preserving the well-being of the organization.

Once again, Eric Liddell's famous run in the 1924 Olympic games comes to mind. To the people in the stands, all the runners appeared equal through the first three-quarters of the race—all bunched together, no one particularly tired or stressed, muscles all working about the same. In good times, even normal periods, most companies do well, regardless of operating styles and philosophies.

Positive market forces can mask festering cancers and vulnerabilities within an organization.

In the last quarter of the race, when the runners were laboring and their leg muscles began tightening up, Liddell began to separate himself from the rest by calling on his reserves. He may not have led all runners at the three-quarter point, but what mattered most was who led at the end, who emerged the winner at the finish line. The servant leader, like Eric Liddell, draws on personal and organizational reserves to win.

Of course, principles and values are not only important to help you get through the bad times, but also to provide a basis for growth during the good times. Creating consistency, trust, stability, and authenticity within the culture allows your organization to take risks and to initiate change. The only constant in business today is change; but change can have a debilitating effect on people. Employees need handles, like trust and consistency, to hang onto during a change process, even when the changes are clearly in their best interests.

Leading and operating from principles provide a basis for true integrity, growth, and profitability. Such success is not measured so much by a singular point in time, or by a particular event, outcome, or milestone; rather, it is measured along a continuum. Progress may even be sporadic, and the harvest may come in bits and pieces throughout a cycle. But in the final analysis, servant leadership is the only way to transcend the "bottom line" and the best way to build relationships, shape lives, contribute to community, boost self-worth, and provide long-term growth and earnings—in other words, to insure that the grass is greener on your side.

CHAPTER FIFTEEN

The Ultimate Harvest

*Personal service, when it merges into universal
service is the only service worth doing.*
— GANDHI

OVER THE PAST TWO DECADES, we've all observed the deterioration of
moral consciousness in our country. The tradition of "do it because
it's right" has eroded as our society seeks more solutions through economic and legal means. Rapid changes cause us to feel tremendous
fear and insecurity. Moreover, traditional family values have been
replaced with alternative family concepts that have weakened our
spirit of community.

As Charles Handy observes in *The Age of Unreason:* "Choice in
relationships now means that the extended family is not a collection
of aunts, uncles, and cousins, but of stepparents and half brothers and
sisters, or of stepbrothers and sisters with no blood connection at all.
Who will be responsible for an aging step-grandmother, or for the
lonely sibling fallen on hard times? Some hope that new

communities, sharing their homes or their workplaces rather than their parentage, will replace the old networks of the family which were so often riven with secret jealousies and ancient feuds. My own fear is that in the end, shared bricks are not so reliable as shared blood."

Our willingness to reach out into the broader community has diminished. The rapid rise of technology has led to an ever-intensifying level of complexity in our work and even our lives, which makes it difficult for us to cope. It seems that the more we know, the more difficult it becomes to predict outcomes. Further, our pace of life has become more hectic. There's so much rush and hurry, so little time to stop and smell the roses. As we reflect less and as we take on more things to do, quality and focus suffer, peace escapes us, and apathy and hopelessness increase.

In *The Paranoid Corporation,* William A. Cohen and Nurit Cohen write: "Organizations, like people, have distinct personalities and—like people—sometimes get sick. If allowed to go untreated, the illness can cause serious harm, even complete breakdown. Fortunately, just as people can be returned to health, so can companies. When the organization is healthy, it gives its members an inoculation that helps ward off failure. It creates a comfortable work atmosphere that empowers members to do their best."

Doing business is certainly harder today. Global competitiveness has intensified as countries that play by different rules and regulations seem to hold the advantage. (Japan, with its government support system, is just one example.) We must consider many issues before making investments or setting strategies—even before manufacturing and marketing our products. These issues include human resources, health care, the environment, federal trade regulations, and safety, as well as the exogenous pressures of our society's litigiousness.

The Role of Leaders

The role of leaders will continue to change as we try to preserve and develop people as our most valuable assets, and as we try to keep our organizations flexible and responsive to the challenges and uncertainties of the future. We will need to focus more attention on insuring that not only the balance sheet but also the people ledger of the organization has enough reserve, tenacity, and capacity to absorb the shocks of change. If we want our organizations to succeed, we will need to act as servants and reawaken the human spirit so that all employees find joy and meaning in their contributions.

John Scherer reminds us in *Work and the Human Spirit* that companies will be more successful when they look to the human spirit of the organization to solve problems. He admonishes leaders who feel that the next new program, or one more corporate initiative such as employee involvement, reengineering, or total quality management might hold the key to the difference between success and failure. Scherer explains that we've come to a point now where more initiatives will not materially matter. We need to remember that people can usually be trusted to do the right thing, and this basic motivation is more powerful than any management initiative or competitive pressure.

Proper leadership creates a climate where each person can make a difference. Leaders empower others to take action and responsibility, to take risks, to participate in solutions. And like parents who exercise "tough love," leaders need to facilitate, encourage, cajole, and sometimes even push people to take responsibility, to be accountable, and to take the lead. In *Even Eagles Need a Push*, David McNally inspires us to act as leaders when he writes:

> THE EAGLE GENTLY COAXED her offspring toward the edge of the nest. Her heart quivered with conflicting emotions as she felt their resistance to her persistent nudging. "Why does the thrill of soaring have to begin with the fear of falling?" she thought. This ageless question was still unanswered for her.
>
> As in the tradition of the species, her nest was located high on the shelf of a sheer rock face. Below there was nothing but air to support the wings of each child. "Is it possible that this time it will not work?" she thought. Despite her fears, the eagle knew it was time. Her parental mission was all but complete. There remained one final task—the push.

The eagle drew courage from an innate wisdom. Until her children discovered their wings, there was no purpose for their lives. Until they learned how to soar, they would fail to understand the privilege it was to have been born an eagle. The push was the greatest gift she had to offer. It was her supreme act of love. And so one by one she pushed them, and they flew!

Ultimately, however, any person's feelings of power or happiness, their motivation or their desire to take initiative must come from within themselves, not from others.

In most organizations, people still operate as if the leader runs the business—in effect, as if the leader is the engine that drives the company. Employees must take more responsibility and be held more accountable. But for them to do so, their sense of ownership must increase. Leaders must allow employees to have real ownership in what they do and what they're responsible for. And this should be genuinely and pervasively applied at all levels, not only at the senior management level.

In *Stewardship,* Peter Block reminds us of the original meaning of that word—protecting the kingdom for the king who is under age or temporarily absent. In modern organizations, this means to preserve and enhance the assets of the corporation for the next generation, and more specifically, to create and sustain an environment for personal as well as corporate growth. Steward leaders find their motivation not only in building profitability and shareholder value, but also in creating and guiding a vision. Stewardship requires leaders to be accountable to the community as well as to the corporation, which means building an organization that is both trustworthy and trusting. Stewardship transforms leadership to a new level.

Personal Reflection

In order to write this book, I have had to think through my convictions. In the process, not only have I learned much but my convictions have been considerably strengthened. For me, it has been a personal journey that has borne much fruit. As I assess Toro's and my own performance against many challenges—including continued growth, acquisitions, consolidations, recessions, and financial recoveries—I must confess that our scores are well below perfect, but I am grateful and proud that the people at Toro responded so effectively and uniformly, moving the company through its problems toward growth and economic health.

I have learned, often the hard way, that human behaviors and styles are deeply rooted, and so fundamental change (real conversion) comes slowly. Since people's personalities and backgrounds differ widely, leadership consistency, repetition, and stability are very important. I've also learned that unleashing a team to pursue external goals, such as customer satisfaction, will generate more positive energy and contribution than you can imagine. Employees are adults, just like leaders, and can usually find the best solutions on their own. In addition, I am aware that employees want to know the truth about what's going on. They can handle the bad news. If they trust you, the team mentality will stay intact even through the crises.

Much patience is required to build a culture of trust. You must first create a clear picture of your expectations, and then firmly, fairly, patiently work with your team. Working with people, getting many involved, taking time to reflect, all create opportunities for improvement. It's all in your people; the trick is to recognize the potential and to provide the positive environment, systems, and process.

Building value from within, as an approach to an organization, is not a new, nor infrequent, direction leaders take. When I first began my career, I remember reading Peter Drucker's exhortation, in one of his early books, to focus on people's strengths and to make them productive. But in my business experience, organizational servitude in order to build an environment for personal growth is uncommon. There are exceptions, to be sure, and the number of examples will hopefully grow, but much more predominant is the view that an employee's role is exclusively to further the goals of the enterprise. As I have awakened to the possibilities and potential of people's growth and contribution beyond achieving an earnings-per-share target, I have chosen to follow a path not traveled by many. As

Robert Frost concluded in his well-known poem, *The Road Not Taken:*

> Two roads diverged in a wood, and I—
> I took the one less traveled by,
> And that has made all the difference.

Servant leadership has been a most gratifying road for me to travel. And it has, indeed, made all the difference.

As I end this part of my journey, I'm aware that I am beginning another. On this new path, I bring new wisdom and insight to seed and shape the many harvests yet to come. I hope this book serves not only as a valuable learning experience on your journey, but also as a call to action. I express my confidence in you, the reader, that you can draw on new leadership, renewed conviction, and timeless principles to seed your future harvests.

Index